I0420009

Published by      :  NYAMEAMA Consult
Book Design by  :  Dennis Amoah Antwi
Edited by           :  Anthony Amoako
Proofreading     :  Kasim Muniru Esq.
Cover Design     :  Nicholas Abakah

ISBN-13: 978-1519647917
ISBN-10: 1519647913

**Available from:**

Amazon and Other Online / Book Stores
And on Kindle and Other devices.

**email:** arnoldboateng@gmail.com

*What evil men must do to move the world on its current journey to anarchy and disaster would be done. That is assured. For centuries, they have seldom failed. What is in doubt is what good men must do to stop them and move the world on a journey to harmony and peace. If good men fail to rise up and evil continues to tighten its grip, Man should not question the God of Heaven for allowing disaster to be the food of mortals on Earth. Man has the power.*

# Acknowledgement

*To GOD be the Glory for His bestowed favours, graces and wealth on me;*

*Many thanks to Rev Edward Antwi, House of Grace Church, Kumasi, Ghana, I appreciate your guidance and fatherhood;*
*To my brothers and Pastors Safa Duah, Bismark Gyamfi and Adasi, I say I appreciate your prayers;*

*Profound gratitude to my mother, Afia Acheampomaa, who took me to the House of GOD, loved me, taught me and fought for me;*
*Thanks to my late father, Anthony Mensah, who told me, "...Knowledge is your key."*

*Most grateful to my wife Irene Acheampong, for her patience and understanding in moments of stress and seclusion;*
*And to my son and daughter for missed weekends out and play times. I would make up to you Herbert and Aseda.*

*I am sincerely grateful to Dennis Amoah, Desk Koncepts; Anthony Amoako, Morning Star School; Kasim Muniru Esq. Nicholas Abakah, Data7 Technologies and Ernest Adu Owusu for your generous contributions towards this work in your unique ways. God bless you all. I am grateful to have met you all. I am also most grateful to all Students and Teachers.*

## Dedication

*I dedicate this book to all Teachers of Humanity; the past, present and those would rise tomorrow to educate man. This work is for these rare souls whose dream was and is, to see the light of love and harmony shine in the hearts of men and this world.*

# TABLE OF CONTENT

Acknowledgement..................................................................iii

Dedication..........................................................................iv

## Chapter 1 8-27

*Hear the cries of the needy*
*So that the Mother who gave birth to all and fills the universe,*
*Would hear you when you cry to Her. Look beyond your needs;*
*Look beyond your family and embrace the human family.*
*In this, you would find warmth which wealth, false gods or the flesh*
*could not bequeath.*

## Chapter 2 28-34

*There is no greater gift than that which is hidden within you.*
*That is God's gift to you for the duration of your natural life.*
*Seek it and you shall find a foundation.*
*Develop it and you shall find peace*

## Chapter 3 35-48

*The messenger comes home tomorrow*
*Prepare his rewards and a banquet*
*Has he not earned them, as every servant must?*

## Chapter 4 49-59

*O LORD, let the righteous find rest in you.*
*Let them remain in you*
*even as the claws of this life dig deep to their souls*
*on this perilous journey called earth.*
*Let him who trusts in you find fulfilment.*
*Let him drink from the milk of Mother Earth*
*In abundance and without measure.*

## Chapter 5             60-69

*"I have suffered...*
*" Yes, you have seen much pain.*
*But have you suffered to the point where pain does not exist?*

## Chapter 6             70-75

*There is no greater evil than that committed by the government*
*and leaders of men:*
*There is no greater misfortune*
*than that permitted by good men and the masses.*

## Chapter 7             76-81

*Two dots could be joined; three dots could be joined;*
*All dots could be joined.*
*It is human regulations and nuances*
*Which make it impossible to join certain dots.*

## Chapter 8             82-91

*I spent years indoors, creating my future;*
*And when I got out of my prison,*
*I started building that future.*
*There was nothing that I was able to build*
*Which I did not build indoors first.*

## Chapter 9             92-98

*The end always comes to everyone.*
*Handle your descent with dignity*
*As much as you embraced your ascent gloriously;*
*For that is the way of all men.*
*We reach our heights and fall.*
*What matters most,*
*and not decided by the Most High, is how you descend;*
*Whether in Grace or disgrace.*

## Chapter 10             99-104

*Train yourself to see beyond pretences,*
*To capture every detail and be able to mesh through good and evil.*
*For on your journey of life, you would meet them at every turn*

*and on each occasion, you would have to make a protracted*
*choice to overcome, lest you would be devoured by the journey,*
*which surely you must make if you are to be remembered.*

## Chapter 11

105-110

*Hear the voice of peace and yield,*
*Hear the tales of glory from the mouth of Him who lived it,*
*And be satisfied with the promise of The MOST HIGH GOD.*
*That, true freedom exists and it is available to all men;*
*It is a freedom which neither hunger, anxiety,*
*torture nor death can overcome.*

## Chapter 12

111-116

*There is a land called love;*
*there is a land called honesty;*
*there is a land called hope;*
*Live in these lands and you would be*
*In the Council of God*

## Chapter 13

117-120

*"It is finished." It is done.*

## Chapter 14

121-126

*Root yourself in the faith of God....*
*...that He lives and answers the prayers of his children*
*and all who cry onto him...*

## Chapter 15

127-130

*Let us protect our rivers,*
*Let us protect our air,*
*Let us protect our forests,*
*Let us build more forests and their ecosystems.*
*Let us protect the land we eat from.*
*They are our primary guardians*

## Chapter 16

131-137

*By the laws of men you live and poured out evil against your*
*brother.Why do you now invoke the laws of God: "love, forgiveness,*

*generosity..."*
*when your brother decides to live by the laws of men as well?*
*Why do you hold the wise in contempt, when he says,*
*"You reap what you sow?"*

## Chapter 17                                         138-145

*Burn the fats; never stop till you reach your goals*

## Chapter 18                                         146-149

*Ignorance of the invisible lines,*
*leads you to the doors of poverty, slavery and frustrations*

## Chapter 19                                         150-154

*Seek greater heights.*
*Seek loftier goals.*
*Claim higher grounds.*
*They are your rights as God's Child.*

## Chapter 20                                         155-160

*Sometimes all it takes to heal body and soul, is a good music*

## Chapter 21                                         161-168

*I owe no debt to the god of religion...*
*The MOST HIGH GOD holds my debts.*
*He sets out the freedom and salvation of all without colour or airs.*
*That by religion, my brother who is the blood of my father and the fluid*
*of my mother*
*Has become my enemy,*
*A hatred creature because he is a Muslim, Christian or Hindu?*

## Chapter 22                                         169-173

*From today, I cease to be responsible for others' wealth*
*And irresponsible to myself.*
*From today, I turn the lights to my well being;*
*I create greatness for myself;*
*I make myself the lord of wealth.*
*I decree them*

*and humbly,*
*I shall be presented to the Throne of Destinies,*
*at the feet of the Ancient of Days*
*For canonisation*

## Chapter 23    174-181

*If I picked paupers and made them millionaires,*
*I can make myself a billionaire.*
*I make myself a billionaire at this hour now and here.*
*My hands are blessed; my intentions for riches are noble.*
*I hope to stand noble till the end of my days.*

## Chapter 24    182-190

*If you can help people who depend on you to climb the Kilimanjaro,*
*Then you can climb the Everest by the hand of fortune*

## Chapter 25    191-195

*I am not my son.*
*My son is not me.*
*But one thing I know:*
*I trained him so well;*
*I taught him the ways of life*
*and I trained him to be a good leader.*

## Chapter 26    196-202

*Live and let us live. Die and let us live....*
*To die or to live depends on the will of MAN.*
*God is forever a benevolent Judge.*

## Chapter 27    203-205

*Have pity on those trapped by their ambitions.*
*Slaves are better off.*

## Chapter 28    206-211

*If you choose to go with the multitude on the common and easy path,*
*you are likely to be as common as the path you have taken.*

**Chapter 29**          212-218

*God gave truth to man.*
*Man turned the truth into a weapon,*
*Not to defend the truth but to attack the truth,*
*So that the masses would continue to be in slavery.*
*Is it the error of God or the test of God?*

**Chapter 30**          219-225

*In a game of Chess, if you hear "checkmate",*
*do not disrupt the game.*
*Be a sportsman;*
*accept your position and play your best move;*
*There is always another game to play.*

**Chapter 31**          226-240

*No one would build your house for you.*
*Dream again..*
*...Build your lands.*
*Build your infrastructures;*
*Stop this senseless materialism;*
*Love your youth.*
*O Africa.*

Index.................................................................................241-263

*The crusades of men against the Truth have never succeeded and they would never do. Little men in their little minds say, "The truth is buried forever" because they have pushed fear into someone or sent messages?" They would bury her but she would only be for a while; they may kill her but she would rise with seven heads; they may suppress her but she would grow stronger and stranger under the layers of falsehood, then, she would sprout out and expose them who have built their world on falsehood.*

*Yes, truth would open the gates of freedom to them who seek her and like a flood, they would storm to the city of liberty; On her wings they would fly through to city of light to enjoy the food of happiness.*

*Truth does not live in the timelines of mortals; She lives in lofty gel of Love, perpetually stable in the fluid of Time… The truth does not limit herself to the pitiful short span of mortals; She leaves in immortality: immovable and timeless.*

*The LORD MOST HIGH GOD would re-establish His truth and no wisdom could withstand it. No big announcements would herald it, yet the Truth would be born, swell and swallow. The light of the true light of God would herald His truth and it shall not slow, It shall not slumber; it shall not falter. Purposefully, every mountain would be levelled, every pretention shall be consumed and falsehoods exposed. Those who seek would find her and be free*

*Men of valour shall become children. They would wail and gnash their teeth and shall seek to hide from the truth of the day, but there would be no darkness anywhere to receive them.*

*The struggle for freedom bellows fear, but strives on. The seeker shouts from pains and irritations, yet he must push on because he knows that the power to live a free and a righteous living would deliver him and establish itself. So plough and crawl on all four, forward and upwards.*

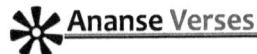 

*May the chosen ones have the courage to tell the message.*
*May God's children see and behold the immeasurable truth of Him*
*whom they serve and give devotion to Him in a life of beauty and purity*
*thus sending a pleasing aroma throughout the earth, reaching even the*
*heavens.*

*May the Warriors of the MOST HIGH GOD finally rise.*

*"It is finished."*
*Yes, it was finished long before the words, "It is finished" were spoken.*

*Someone's Angel is another man's Devil.*
*Someone's freedom is another man's incarceration in a tent of fear and anxiety.*
*Someone's friend is another man's enemy...*

*The End would eventually come;*
*It is already here.*

As I write Ananse Verses,
I see smoke, hear of terrors across continents
and behold murderous drives of refugees on television and radio;
Shadows appearing and disappearing
and the pitiful struggles of little men holding on to falsehood to enslave
God's Children.
They are men who do not know that the battle is over.
Yes, the battle was over long before their mortal bodies were born.
Their lord and lords have already abandoned ship and sent the retreat
signal.
Their emissaries are out and up there in dark patches negotiating for
truce, mercy and pardon.

*Today you bully the children because you can;*
*What would you do when they come to know that*
*it is not about the muscles and blood, but the brain and the power of it*
*What would you do when they come to know that,*
*they are wiser than you are and more powerful?*
*What would you do when they come to know that they can command*
*you to be their servants? I can only say this, "Prepare for your*
*nightmare."*

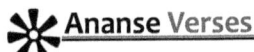
# Chapter

*Hear the cries of the needy*
*So that the Mother who gave birth to all and fills the Universe,*
*Would hear you when you cry to Her. Look beyond your needs*
*Look beyond your family and embrace the human family*
*In this, you would find warmth which wealth, false gods or the flesh*
*could not bequeath*

1. Justice exists for yesterday, today and tomorrow;
    1.1. Justice, which does not serve itself is no justice at all.
    1.2. In his wholeness, it is a form of God touching many phases of time in the life of every society,
    1.3. And dispensing order and fairness through wisdom for the protection of mortals in our many needs.
    1.4. If there is any taint, it is by our flawed nature and not of Justice's essence.
    1.5. Justice is for the weak as well as the strong.
    1.6. Justice protects the weak from the strong and protects the strong from himself.
    1.7. Eventually, through Justice's success, we are all protected.
    1.8. Therein lies the wisdom for all, that we should uphold it, protect it and tolerate its flaws.
    1.9. Without it, we would have only strong men and weak men.
    1.10. In such a world, we shall have anarchy on our hands and society shall not survive.
    1.11. Do we need laws without Justice or Justice without written laws?
    1.12. Or can laws exist without Justice or Justice without laws?
    1.13. Does the presence of laws guarantee Justice?
    1.14. Should we not say, "Hail selfishness" for the sake of Justice?
    1.15. Hail Justice; hail his defenders; hail those who receive his lashes and favours; hail those it offends.
    1.16. Can Justice exist and flourish without the Police Service to lead combatants to his house?
    1.17. Can Justice exist without the Military to tower over stubborn elements and send a clear message of brute force if they avoid Justice?
    1.18. Or is it not possible for brute force to exist as a by-product of certain forms of Justice?
    1.19. Can Justice exist without the Intelligence Services to establish drills?

1.20. Without the Idea of a Nation or a human family, can Justice even exist?

1.21. In all, we have chains of actors, receivers and mourners.

1.22. In this, can we say that without the highest form of honesty, dignity and integrity, Justice cannot find its true voice?

1.23. Let there be sanity.

1.24. Let the society continue to believe that Justice shall not bow to any wish other than itself and its publicised tenets,

1.25. May the society continue to see Justice untainted, unravelled and unbent.

1.26. O Justice, make us believe in you perpetually.

1.27. On this earth, should we seek the Justice of God or the rod of man resting on the whims of the powerful?

1.28. We seek the Justice of God, knowing that the flaws of man shall inhibit it.

1.29. Yet, we shall be happy with whatever results Justice bequeaths us, reckoning that without even the worse form of Justice we shall all go up in flames in hailstorms of anarchy.

1.30. Herein the society shall rise and watch any who has a lever of Justice in the hand carefully.

1.31. That, he should dispense the little powers with care, love, honesty and fairness.

1.32. Lest the Idea of Justice is slandered and assassinated.

1.33. If Mercy is not found in the hands of any who holds a lever of Justice, the society shall not be upset.

1.34. If leniency is not accommodated in the tents of any who holds a lever Justice, the society shall not die. It shall grow stronger.

1.35. Chivalry shall not be in the character of any of his runners.

1.36. It is all about Justice for yesterday, today and tomorrow for the sake of man and for the growth and survival of the society we have created or shall so create.

2. Those who call evil into their homes would become the slaves of it.

   2.1. O if we knew the evil we have called forth into our homes;

   2.2. If we knew the coming storms;

   2.3. If we knew the coming frosts, darkness and fires we would have started the run for the hills.

   2.4. Cities would be laid waste.

   2.5. Rivers would turn stagnant with rotten flesh;

   2.6. Bunkers would be the grave of the mighty who claim to be gods;

   2.7. Messengers would not overcome the celestial blockades;

   2.8. Those whose ships would ascend the heavens would float into oblivion.

   2.9. Yes, then we would wish we had kept this beauty called Earth; nourished and protected her.

   2.10. Perception would destroy us;

   2.11. Curiosity would obliterate us;

   2.12. Pride would smash us against unknown rocks and break us into pieces.

   2.13. What are we doing to ourselves?

3. O Religion, what a weapon! There is the religion of Salvation and the religion of power, control and domination. Which one is or would be at play in your life? You are the only one who knows or would allow.

4. Devotion, Obsession and madness are all parts of the human story;

   4.1. I am obsessed with my dreams so I read and struggle all day;

   4.2. I am obsessed with wisdom so I seek the old and wise all day;

   4.3. I am obsessed with wealth for the good of my family so I seek favour and grace and perfect my thoughts all day;

   4.4. I am obsessed with power for the good of my Mother so I seek humility and contentment all day. I would not be consumed by it, lest I lose my beauty and path.

4.5.   These I seek. They blind me. Day and night, I groan. All my might is on them.

4.6.   I break down several times in a day because of these obsessions.

4.7.   I have body pains because of them.

4.8.   I am a tortured soul, with neither peace nor rest.

4.9.   In all, I look to the Most High God for he has told me my consuming ambition would be rewarded.

4.10.  To Him I give devotion for wisdom, dreams, health and wealth.

5.   What we say and do in private, if they were to be made public, would reduce many of us to children. Thousands would go to jail; millions to hell and the world would come to an abrupt end.

6.   If you fight someone else's battle for him, you take the blows meant for him. Mind your affairs. When you seek to fight for the oppressed and the weak, do the noble thing by teaching them how to fight their own battles.

7.   There is a proper procedure for doing everything. If you go wayward, however noble your intensions are, you would be accused before the elders and they would not absolve you.

8.   Every dream is within reach. Every vision is achievable. With your eyes in your head, follow the dreams of your childhood religiously and you shall blossom.

9.   Look at the World for what it is and not as you wish it to be or dream of it in your beautiful mind. The world is cold. It has no place for children , the weak or the too powerful. This World is real.

10.  Today, I am creating the tomorrow I want. I would walk into it and as I step into it, I would remind myself that I created it yesterday.

11. Young children, Ananse advises; "Whatever you are doing, consider it as a route to your dreams and not only as a means of earning a certificate or a monthly salary or worse, to please someone." You are the only one who can create who you want to be. If it is beyond you, The ELOHIM would give strength.

12. There is a price for every dream. There are as many prices as there are dreams. Tell me your dream and I would tell you the price to be paid;

12.1. Einstein, Emerson, Antha Diop, Kwame Nkrumah and all our luminaries, see how happy and great we think they were.

12.2. They paid their price, played their roles, fulfilled their roles and departed.

12.3. Their fears we remember not,

12.4. Their tears we care not about,

12.5. Their faults we trumpet day and night.

12.6. They lived, fulfilled and departed.

12.7. The rest was for the scavengers to feed on their leftovers and sell themselves to poor mortals as great men.

12.8. The composers were the great men. The actors are not.

13. Keep growing for what gives you joy, motivation and satisfaction today may annoy you tomorrow. Growth and maturity have a way of embarrassing you when you look back.

14. In order to achieve your dreams, you need to seek to understand your environment; identify how to develop your potentials and search for the sacrifices required of you.

15. There is always a reason; there is a reason for every action, even if the reason is stupid. Ananse says there are seven levels of reasons, but he mentioned only three; "the one we tell the public; the other, we tell our close confidants and the third, the one which we keep to ourselves, never to be even whispered."

16.  Dreams should rest on reality and their attainment, on hard skills. Nothing grandiose; nothing careless; nothing glorious; nothing on a silver platter.

17.  Things you work hard for, you fight hard enough to keep; things you pick up easily, you may lose through carelessness.

18.  Ananse's charge to his son is, "My son, know that, I love you above all else. Know that you are my light. You inspired me to this house. I would live to see you live the promise, and I sing with joy to the Most High. For He is great above all else. Only this I ask of you: "fear God, purify your passions and serve humanity."

19.  At the end of the day, when you say you have achieved your dream, there should be something meaningful or physical to show for it. Let us remember that.

20.  I crave for peace in my house. I strive with all my energies to preserve that peace. I work hard to make it a Temple, for it houses my body, which is the temple of God.

21.  Yes, we are an extension of Him who created and breathed into our nostrils. So let us live holy and righteous lives.

22.  There comes a time you would have to swallow a lot of nonsense from both high and low. Do not forget that. Remember that those times would not last forever. Once lessons have been learnt, you would grow on and with that growth, comes your freedom and satisfaction.

23.  Why is your head bowed? Lift your head up and swallow the nonsense, the humiliations and the spikes of the arrogant in their illusions. Let their slurs and their low words energise you to strive high. With time, you would achieve your goals. By this, you would have dignity and a place in your heart to be proud of how well you have done for yourself.

24.  "Look at how great it has become. It was only a simple dream. We started in someone's storeroom and failed. We never gave

up. We paid our price, prepared and came back. It was the madness of passion. Now look at what it has become. Great dreams sometimes start small."

25. Everything is in the hands of God, who has set the Universe in place with laws, lines, doors and presence, seeing everything, listening and responding to all in the measure we respond and relate to him. May the children grow; may the wise learn more; may the teachers teach the purity of His voice; may we all know as we are enabled.

26. God is to us as we see him. To those who know him as God, he is God; to those who know him as LORD OF HOSTS, He is so. Nothing more, nothing less. Ananse says: "God is The Master of all and LORD over the Universe. He creates, reforms and prepares His vessels for His work. Your view of Him does not make Him less or more."

27. "Why did you waste such resources, or did or did not do this or that?" You think an intelligent man would take an action without thinking? Ask for his reasons and learn. Refuse and you are simply a simplistic and arrogant bull blabbering around for attention.

28. What the eye does not see is far greater than what it does;
28.1. Trust is a currency. It could be quantified in material terms. It costs the giver so do not take trust for granted nor abuse it.
28.2. To the politician, the trust given to you by voters could be quantified and returned by building roads, hospitals, and schools;
28.3. To the Chief Executive, the trust of shareholders is the rise in share values and corporate responsibility
28.4. To the parent, the trust of the family is food, accommodation and protection.
28.5. To all humanity, the trust given in whatever endeavour, is to give love in return.

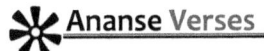 

29.    The Master's touch is unmistakable and always reliable.

29.1.  Sometimes you go softly,

29.2.  At other times you go strongly.

29.3.  You cannot always go in strongly; you cannot always go in softly.

29.4.  Sometimes you cease to exist.

29.5.  Knowing the right combinations and the right time calls for wisdom, which only the Master possesses.

29.6.  How else would you separate the Master from the boys, children and those bragging crusaders?

30.    Create a problem you can solve. Do not create a problem and expect someone to clean it up for you. Ananse says, "That is reckless and irresponsible. And there is a price to pay."

31.    You have handled War heroically; let us see how you would handle the Peace. Many great war heroes have failed to handle the peace time, and with that failure came their misfortune.

32.    Power acquired gradually over a long period is the most formidable and when wisely used, becomes a weapon for good and wealth creation.

33.    Show me someone who has taken a major leap in life without his share of troubles, and I would show you "smoke without fire" or a forest without undergrowth.

33.1.  Troubles come in succession in those moments of trials and tests,

33.2.  But the blessings trickle in, moving slowly at tortoise pace unless THE ELOHIM decides otherwise.

33.3.  Troubles come without warnings; so are the blessings unannounced even if you sense them.

33.4.  Restoration has his hour

33.5.  When we have gone through our trials, and if we overcome we are lifted to higher states and grounds of honour and dignity.

33.6.  This is the journey the MOST HIGH has set for all mortals.

33.7. Those who abide by this order, triumph and journey to purity;

33.8. Those who refuse may rise but would fall to lesser beings.

34. Words have voice; words have power; words have life and, of course, death in their nodes.

34.1. They are real as the human is real.

34.2. They are potent as the sword of the warrior is;

34.3. They are destructive as the tornadoes of the Bermuda;

34.4. They are as healing as the breezes of fulfilment.

34.5. The right words in the hands of the Master is ultimate power the Divine could bestow on a mortal

35. You said there were no weapons there. Yes, I said that. But he has shot me three times. No, I said there were weapons but those weapons could not harm you. Really? He has shot me and I am dying. Really? You were a fool to trust me. Ananse says, "Trust your wisdom first and foremost. All else is chance, fate, destiny and luck if The Divine has no direct hand in the events."

36. The Worlds of men, gods and God are unique, parallel and conjoined:

36.1. The world runs on principles, values, rules, lines and vectors.

36.2. The world does not run on the impulses of any persons.

36.3. It is madness for someone to think that it runs on a group of mortals holed up in a bunker. It is a delusion created to enslave poor mortals who deserve what is coming because they believed.

36.4. They succeed by experiments as we also do.

36.5. The Most High watches and decides.

36.6. In the meantime, O man, go beyond;

36.7. Reach for the hallowed realms where no lines, vectors, principles or rules exist.

36.8. Reach out to the grounds where holiness, and light reigns.

36.9. Reach out to that realm where dirt, rot or your earthly lords cannot even glimpse.

36.10. And you shall be lord of your path and journey

36.11. On the day you make the decision to reach out, they would not only loathe you, but would make rocky your path but you would receive the gift of grace, glory, acceptance and power to overcome.

36.12. Mad they would grow; battles they would declare on you; their swords would wound you but you would grow stronger and journey to the end.

36.13. Knowing this, O man, let your sun embrace the eternal sun of the Most High God so that in your oneness, you would cause those who have chosen to live in the lower realms in greed, wickedness, hate and wars to rise to higher realms.

37. Man the divine; man the mortal; man the creature; man the creator. Whoever you are, it must be for the good of Mother Earth and the Universe.

37.1. O Man, reach out to the heavens where you belong;

37.2. O man, reach out to what is love, righteous and holy. These are the emblems of your home.

37.3. O man, leave this tent behind and ascend to the realms of light.

37.4. O man, why do you allow yourself to be trapped by this tent called blood and flesh?

37.5. It is only a borrowed garment to aid your existence on Planet Earth.

37.6. Wake up you are divine.

37.7. Thrive home and let those who come from afar see the holiness of your father.

38. Survivors, thieves and looters we all are.

38.1. When you take for your survival, you are not a thief; because you are fulfilling your God-given right to survive;

38.2. When you take for pleasure or fun, you are a thief, because you have not been deprived of your right of survival. You are simply wasting what is meant for someone.

38.3. When you take from the public for pleasures and passions, you heap piles of curses on yourself and your descendants.

38.4. These are not the babblings of Ananse. These are the words of Wisdom that "we should not waste; we should not deny the poor of his right to food, shelter and survival."

39. Have you paid the price? Have you earned the right to the seat upon which you sit? Have you surrendered to the Most High? Welcome home and blow your boasts:

39.1. I have paid the price.

39.2. I have believed the MOST HIGH.

39.3. I have walked the journey.

39.4. Let me be proud of what I have done for myself.

39.5. Let me kill all my enemies for I have overcome their weapons.

39.6. Let me take my vengeance on them, and their collaborators and their admirers.

39.7. None should pity them.

39.8. They brought misfortune onto themselves when they set out to destroy an innocent man.

39.9. Leave every hero to his fate.

39.10. Let him enjoy his moments.

39.11. Let him write his own legend to gloat in his fleeting glories.

39.12. After all, what matters is the Chronicles of the MOST HIGH. It has every deed, truthfully recorded.

39.13. How else can a resting warrior find pleasure than to occasionally boast about his elementary achievements?

39.14. Give room to conquerors, after all they have conquered something.

40. Dreams and reality, so close yet eternity apart.

40.1. Be careful when crossing the bridge between dreams and reality.

40.2. It is not that simple.

40.3. It is not that easy.

40.4. It is real work.

40.5. The reality is different.

40.6. Watch your steps; count them accordingly and

40.7. Let the wise interpret them to you accordingly.

41. Ananse cautions that, "You little men who sit in your little rooms and judge everything, beware because very soon the sun would set on you, and when it does, you would look back and find out that you have spent all your days talking about other people without doing anything for yourselves. Your food, from then on till you pass on, would be bitterness and regrets."

42. Do you seek to be fit for divine use?

42.1. Prepare your body for heaven;

42.2. Prepare your body for the spirit of the Most High.

42.3. Prepare your mind and body for the Holy Spirit, that He may give you strength and teach you the ways of this material world and of this Universe.

42.4. Keep your body healthy,

42.5. Do not eat excessive food,

42.6. Do not drink poison,

42.7. Do not put substances into your body, which would make you unhealthy.

42.8. Is it not a sin to poison God's temple?

42.9. Is it not a sin to disobey the hallowed voice of The Most High?

42.10. Is it not a sin to hold dark matters like greed, hate, envy and impatience in your body even if they surge from your mind?

42.11. Clear your mind of all dark matter and you would be healthy and fit for divine use.

42.12. Does not envy and the family of bitterness, greed, pride and fear poison your body and soul?

43. Irresponsibility has a price. Do not think there is someone somewhere who would perpetually pledge absolution for your follies. Do you think your next follies and mess would come crushing on someone else's head

again? He is gone. The mess you create would come crushing on your head. Grace absolved the early follies.

44. Words of the Epiphyte: "I pray for you my boss. I pray for your good health and long life, not because I love or care about you but because your misfortunes would be a great material loss to me." Then the boss replied: "I would make your life more dependent upon me so that you do not become independent of me because I value your prayers."

45. When the child asks, "When would this end?" We tell him, "When you grow up." But the wise knows that it does not end. It only gets tougher as you grow or transforms itself into other forms. So prepare yourself for the future and arm yourself with knowledge and foresight.

46. The frustrations of a noble Mother:
46.1. Mother Africa weeps at the folly of her children;
46.2. She weeps at the cowardice of her Shepherds;
46.3. She bows her head in shame among the Mothers.
46.4. She would have the last Word; yes, Mother Africa would have the last laugh.
46.5. Her head would be lifted up higher when her golden generations arrive and march to victories and home.
46.6. She would sing the songs of victory.
46.7. Joy would fill her heart and her cheeks would glow.
46.8. She would march to the throne of glory and reverence and who can behold her beauty?
46.9. Within the circles she dances and in her right arm she holds the lamp to direct the path of her children.
46.10. Whether our legacy has been stolen or borrowed, it does not matter now. She has risen
46.11. Mother Africa is beautiful and majestic.
46.12. Who can muster the right words to describe her poise?
46.13. Grace is her name.
46.14. Her eyes are full of wisdom.

46.15. Lesser mothers chase after her wisdom; jealous and ashamed in her presence.

46.16. One gaze from her and they jump in the air with satisfaction all their lives.

46.17. If only her children would know her, how great they would be!

46.18. Her eyes radiate so much wisdom that whatever she gazes upon is turned into gold.

46.19. Mother Africa, mother of gods, builders, inventors, teachers of science and mathematics and sages.

46.20. Mother Africa is the Mother among mothers.

46.21. Mother Earth weeps more bitterly.

47. He is waiting for you. Come back all you who sold your souls to this world cheaply for fame, paper wealth and materials. Come to the LIGHT and The SOVEREIGN LORD and LORD of HOSTS. The door is open but for a brief time.

48. Many a good man has died for their good hearts, for their good intentions and the light in their eyes. So do not live your life in the error that, you are invincible. Know the times; know the doors; know the lines and count your steps.

49. The folly of fools or the folly of the arrogant? When they perceive favourable end results, they say, "We are smart. Our strategy worked." But when it turns out badly, they would find themselves a blame goat. When they fail because they failed to perceive the battle, they would shout, "We are under the grace of the LORD. The Battle is the LORD's." The LORD only protects those under His wings; Those who trust in Him and not the ignorant or children bloated with poisons.

50. "This is the last war." Ananse says: "You can say that to please yourself." He warns: "Do not delude yourself. There is nothing like the last war. One battle ends and another starts. This is the unfortunate fate we have inherited as warrior mortals."

51. Power is neither a weapon for fools nor to be left to children. The wise knows this and takes what is only necessary for the purpose, but the fool takes and takes until it becomes a curse onto him and finally, he is consumed by it.

52. We are not alone; others to watch us; others to manipulate us; others to teach and guide us; some to protect us; from day to night they work to achieve their missions.

53. If you find a purpose to live for, you would always find the strength to fight on.

53.1. When a nation overcomes her demons and makes peace with her past; when a nation finds her soul and establishes her destiny, she shall rise and when she does, she rises to the skies with hope and purpose. An eventual bliss would be her reward.

53.2. When a person overcomes his demons and makes peace with his past; when he finds his soul and establishes his destiny, if he so wishes, it is all about purpose and bliss;

53.3. When a society overcomes her demons and makes peace with her past; when that society shall accept her guilt and make restitution, she would freely drag herself into a prosperous future without the burdens of past evil deeds hanging around her neck or the neck of her children or be haunted by the demons of yesteryears' deeds.

53.4. When a people refuse to accept their past and confront their demons, they would perpetually live in fear of tomorrow and with this fear would come a burden, which would in their time of rest, disrupt their happiness.

53.5. And so shall any stiff-necked person who refuses to accept his guilt, parts with his evils deeds and embrace the light of truth, good deeds and the good of society be cut off.

54. The Bluffer:

54.1. I am a Colossus.

54.2. I am the dragon slayer.

54.3.  I am who I am because I have the seal of the MOST HIGH.

54.4.  Ananse says you are a bluffer if you claim such unmerited glory.

54.5.  You are the face of what is done but not the Dragon Slayer.

54.6.  The Slayer walks silently in the cool basking in the glory that, he has slayed the Dragon, which haunted Gods children and breathed fire.

54.7.  The Dragon Slayer never talks,

54.8.  He does not crave for the adulations of mortals,

54.9.  He is barely in the sight of fools.

54.10.  Silently he walks and calmly he slays the Dragons.

54.11.  You only sense he was there not from what he says but from the silent glory of his deeds.

54.12.  Out of him, eagles are born;

54.13.  Out of you, Parrots are incubated and hatched, to continue the deafening sounds of emptiness.

55.  Ananse says: "Those children who follow me be careful of where you step because I have wings. Act as your abilities should allow you. Do not act out of ego, arrogance or ambition. Success always measures us by our abilities and graces and not by our ego, or ambition or wish."

56.  Be careful when calling someone a fool. Even a fool would not take it kindly if you call him a fool. Yes, even if you call a fool a fool, he would not be happy with you.

57.  The echoes of achievers are overwhelming, from one milestone to another till Time speaks. You struggle through rain and mud; inflict yourself with mortal wounds; see death several times and bleed till you find your calling which always seems to lie under your nose. Then the battle for acceptance begins; then the battle upwards begins. Then in the throes of vulnerability, you tell yourself, "I am done when this is over. This is the last battle." And when it is over, as surely as change never ceases, you would manage to find another battle, sometimes, bigger than the preceding. Till you find your calling, you would never know

satisfaction; till you find your calling, you would never know fulfilment. Find your calling, it is just beyond your fingertips.

58.   Do you sincerely believe my demise would bring you to inherit what you seem to have perceived in your mind? You are wrong. What you see is an illusion. I am the only one who can bring that illusion to reality. My death is your loss.

59.   I am the pillar. I am the Colossus. All seem easy and simple so you have lost respect and balance. O stupid nations, pray that, you mature before the Colossuses depart, lest you become food for the Dragons. Then you would cry for them but it would be too late.

60.   Truth has her own voice and frequency. It is distinct and unmistakable. She is available to everyone. Those who seek her find her. Her voice can never be confused with any other; so no man has an excuse not to know her.

61.   Grace resides and floats on your steps, O African woman. You give grace colour; you give her fullness; carry yourself with poise and walk majestically on the milky roads of Mother Earth. You are the keeper of wisdom and the Mother of all.

62.   The power of God resides in His WORD and not in religion and its traditions, conventions and structures, lest man is misled and wasted.

63.   Be careful what you get yourself into. Why do you enter into a situation without knowing how to get out of it?

64.   Do not ask for more than you need. Do not look beyond your nose without knowing what lies under it. It is simply a matter of common sense.

65.   Start all over. It is never too late.

66.   Soldiers never sleep; they never even close their eyes; they are the eternal wall of protection and guardians of our economic prosperity. Without them we are exposed and flood of enemies would flood our soil to devour us. We need soldiers.

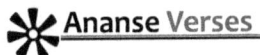 

Where are our soldiers? "I am a soldier in the army of Mother Africa."

67.　To run or to stand your ground. What would you do?

67.1. If you run, you would be hunted down and cut to pieces;

67.2. If you stand your ground you would be cut to pieces.

67.3. What would you do? What should you do?

67.4. O I say, stand and fight like a warrior.

67.5. And if you are to be cut to pieces you would take pride in the fact that you stood and fought.

67.6. This is your victory and the pride of every warrior.

67.7. And I dare say, look into the eyes of your assailants as their swords cut into your flesh.

67.8. If you do, the light of God would flash forth and wage an eternal war on them for your courage and dignity.

68.　Every believer is a warrior. Your weapons are the elements of your Faith.

69.　Give thanks to the GOD of Heaven.

69.1. I thank the GOD of Heaven for all he has done for me.

69.2. I thank Him for this moment of rest.

69.3. I thank Him for this glass of water before me.

69.4. I thank Him for the food in my kitchen.

69.5. I thank Him for the peace in my land.

69.6. I thank Him for the promise of tomorrow.

69.7. I thank Him for this gift of life.

69.8. I thank Him for my family.

69.9. I thank God for all He has promised me.

69.10. I thank the GOD of Heaven for everything.

69.11. This is my gratitude.

70.　Those who created what they created, hold it in disguise till their set time at which they reveal the purpose to which they were created.

70.1. During their journey to their purpose, they perform lots of functions; some good, others open; many coded; always the ultimate goal in focus.

70.2. Then the hour set by the creators arrive and the veil is lifted.

The wise sees the scheme from afar and take steps;

70.3.  The fool watches and dances around it till he is consumed

70.4.  The child sees but does not understand. If he shall survive it, he would ask and be told to gain wisdom

70.5.  By this, next cycle, he would not ask, his wisdom shall sound life into him and he shall be whole.

71.  I bless my Mother for putting the Bible in my hands. I bless whoever put the first book in my hands. I bless whoever built the first classroom, trained the teacher and taught me the alphabets and numerals.

# Chapter

*There is no greater gift than that which is hidden within you. That is God's gift to you for the duration of your natural life. Seek it and you shall find a foundation. Develop it and you shall find peace*

1. The key lies within "The Self", so watch your thoughts;
    1.1. Watch what you feed your mind with, lest you stunt your growth and block your path to greatness.
    1.2. Watch the food you put into your body lest the bridge between your body and soul is corrupted by diseases and illness;
    1.3. Everything lies within.
    1.4. Every problem comes from within.
    1.5. All true and lasting solutions come from within.
    1.6. The salvation of every man lies within.

14 The salvation of every nation lies within her borders. So are her problems.

15 The salvation of every nation and continent lies within her boundaries. So are her challenges.

16 For you to hear clearly and embrace grace, cease all the noise in your mind. If only the noise would cease, you would hear the voice of truth clearly and unfiltered. With it comes health, peace and freedom.

17 Children, out of your abundance you give them a handful, then you test them to give you a dip of it and they refuse. Soon the handful is finished and they run back to you for more. Well, give them again because they are children; but if a wicked man does so, break his neck.

18 Time does miracles. Let the matter pass; let him go; let her go, you would never know what miracle time would spring up just tomorrow.

19 Oh Kaka played well. Yes, Kaka played well. Of course, he played well but remember that Ramires was in the shadows doing the dirty work.

20 When you live with people who do not give, your primary survival skill should be to learn how to take.

21  Plan your life from the beginning to the end. If God were unhappy with any part of it, He would correct it. Leaving your life unplanned, to chance, with the hope that Divinity would hold it true for you, is an insult to God. You are telling Him he was unwise to have given you intellect.

22  To the child, the teacher says: *no one knows the end of the world.* To the wise the teacher says: *know the end of time and live accordingly.*

23  Weapons and Methods of Wars in the battles of men:
23.1  Every war requires its weapons.
23.2  In an unconventional war, the best weapons should be of unconventional origin.
23.3  In an uneven war, the best way to come out alive is through guerrilla methods.
23.4  Material weapons would frustrate you with their annoying limitations but the weapons of Love, Truth, Honesty, Contentment and Balance are eternal and unsurpassable.
23.5  Those whose weapons are these are the lords of eternity. They would never be lost in history nor would their deeds be dwarfed by time.
23.6  Above all, Prayer is the ultimate weapon of all mortals. It creates the P-Bomb to give a medium, which lifts love, truth, honesty and balance beyond the boundaries of men to the realm of divinity and renders them potent beyond, measure destroying all strongholds, pretentions, and barriers.
23.7  These weapons form an indestructible shield over your territories, making you safe beyond measure.
23.8  But how does the P-Bomb acquire its power and runs forth material and spiritual worlds? It is a process only the Wise knows but he is not permitted to utter, not even whisper.
23.9  Simply love, be truthful, honest and be content, hold everything in equal measure and pray.

24  The teacher can only teach the way but it takes the student to take the teachings to heart and walk the way.

It is only by the student walking the path, can he learn and become a better person. In this, the teacher would find fulfilment and rest. That is his reward and his joy.

25 Rarely are heroes born in peacetime. Great men are born, and revealed in times of adversity.

26 Salvation has been turned into bondage under the glorious watch of invincible men;

26.1 Religion and its hierarchies have become deceptions the devil has used to tricked man into deviating us from the true path to maturity and holiness.

26.2 Imagine there is no Roman Catholic Church, no Anglican, no Methodists and nothing at all with our human hierarchies, but that we are all followers of Christ with Christ himself as our guide and leader.

26.3 Imagine there were no Muslims, but all the children of God in a world growing into maturity towards eternity.

26.4 In such an environment, we shall all be known as saints and each of us would be known for who he is and not because of an elected office.

26.5 Then holiness and our worthiness shall be our measure of power and status.

26.6 Everyone would be seen as he is without the intimidation of a false aura surrounding the physical offices of men.

26.7 Then our leaders would emerge, as the LORD shall appoint through his prophets, word of knowledge or revelation.

26.8 Can you imagine how far peace would have travelled in our world by now if religion had not drawn boundaries in our hearts, minds and lands?

26.9 Imagine the nations burnt; the human lives wasted; the famines; the past wars; the eternal wars and the darkness consuming us. All in the name of one great God of religion.

26.10 Let truth and the light of Him shine through us;

26.11 May we, as sons of The Elohim, know the voice of truth and free ourselves from lowness and rise;

26.12 May we be happy and savour the food of truth and eternal light.

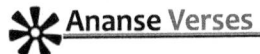

26.13 May we be who we are supposed to be as we crawl to free ourselves and escape into the true Light of God.

27 Everything, every occurrence, every emergence, is part of the divine plan.

28 There have been threats to my life. Many have called to threaten my family, and friends. I do not care a hoot about them. I can deal with them because I now know them. The ones I fear are those who have not spoken. I know they are there, but they have not spoken. I know they have long arms yet they have not shown it. I know they are watching and lurking in the shadows. This is the fear. This is my real fear. I do not know them.

29 There is nothing like betrayal, misfortune or pain. It is part of a process. Look keenly and boldly into them and you would find the gold nuggets only people in your situation can access. And when you find them, use them as tools for the improvement of your life.

30 The right path is never straight. It is winding; it has hills and valleys; you rise and fall; you stumble and sometimes descend its slopes painfully. Joyously embrace the narrow path and plough ahead. On this path you would find yourself. On this path you would meet good fortune. On this path, O man, you would find the strength and maturity to overcome the mud of mortality and strange deceptions. And when you have withstood and overcome, you would be mature and bred for the noble work, which the Most High entrusts to only His precious vessels.

31 The child needs peace. The messenger needs peace. Has he not suffered enough? Has he not honoured The Most High God? Has he not proven his loyalty? We are rewarded as we have honoured our duties. It is a law with divine dimensions.

32 We cannot survive in anarchy. We cannot survive in a society without rules, guidelines and laws. In such a society only the strong survives. Yes, you are strong today so you find comfort in the anarchy and status quo. Would you be strong forever? Remember this and build a society resting solidly on the bedrock of laws, rules and justice. In this, are all safe.

33   The rules of life is that, you know which questions to ask; how
     to ask them; when to ask them. You should know what to know
     and what not to know. You should know which issues to pick,
     which battles to pick and which ones to let go.

34   Lamentations of Ananse:
34.1  I have known humiliation
34.2  I have known disgrace
34.3  I have known pain
34.4  I have known hunger
34.5  And I have known betrayal.
34.6  I hated them all but now I love them.
34.7  They taught me to depend on God and not on my strength.
34.8  I have known failure, not once, not twice. By the time I was
      near my physical prime, I had known several.
34.9  Several times I have resisted training, but like a struggling
      child in the grip of his mother, I was held and led till I came
      to know that, it was all for my good to face the world of
      strange beings ahead of me.
34.10 All is part of the divine to make me ready.
34.11 Today, I stand not only because I am worthy.
34.12 No, I stand because I paid the price.
34.13 I was examined.
34.14 I was refined by fire.
34.15 I was tested and I passed.
34.16 The teachers say I have been proven!
34.17 This is the sacred story of all the greats.
34.18 Let them who boast tell the world they have been tested,
      and proven qualified.

35   The Divine said, "It is finished". The teacher said: "You must
     pay the price." Everybody has to pay the price.

36   In the comfort of my inner world I conceived my visions. Over
     time, I have refined them in the fires, storms and tortures of
     this life. So here I am, a man of great deeds. It was neither by
     chance nor luck.

37 Those who speak of God's grace with neither a purpose in life nor vision and skills, are using the talk of "grace" as an excuse for their laziness and pathetic lives unless they are seeking the "grace-of-vision-and-skills."

38 Come back to God. His bridge of forgiveness and acceptance is still open to you. Run to Him whilst you can. A time may come, that time is not far off when all would be beyond you.

39 Those of you who claim to know GOD; are you sure you do? No, you do not. If you do, you would not worship Satan.

# Chapter

*The messenger comes home tomorrow.*
*Prepare his rewards and a banquet.*
*Has he not earned them, as every servant must?*

1. Some would have their glory through wars; others through nourishing of peace to keep God's children safe and secured, saving them from apprehension and anxieties. And many, if not a few, would have their glory through wisdom. Ananse says that, "Time dictates all and the Universe would be in agreement."

2. There is always a limit to everything. The wise would know that limit and halt. The fool would rumble on till he gets himself into all sorts of pain, and finally loses everything.

3. When wealth is in your control, it does not matter how you acquired it; what matters is what it is used for. When acquiring wealth, it matters how you acquired it. For in the end, even though man would not remember how it was acquired, God would not forget the path you took, the harm you caused and the tears you left in your trail.

4. Hold your talents true and match them with strength, dedication and dignity. Be true to them and they would bring you honour and fulfilment. Without them, you would not realise the full blast of God's blessings.

5. If you rush you would lose everything; if you rush, you would miss your stop; if you rush, you would miss the opportunities along your way. Carefully count your steps and allow the winds of grace and patience to direct and guide you on the path of life.

6. Whatever the circumstances do not embrace greed. If you do, you risk losing everything. Do not get greedy. If you do, you would lose everything.

7. Sometimes it is about the money. Sometimes it is about the Brand. If it becomes a matter of which one to choose first, Ananse says choose Brand. With brand money would follow. Using money to buy brand is very possible but it is an uphill task, which would not last even when achieved - an avoidable burden.

8. Evolution and revolution both result in change. They are simply matters of rate, time and effects.

9. If God gives you wisdom, beauty, intellect and grace, do not be in haste to rush to the world. Wait till you have the strength to protect them. Lest you would become food for the ugly wolves out there in this ugly world. And in the end you would curse God for your misfortune. But remember that, God cannot be blamed for your haste. Patience is the sacred virtue, which can lead you through all gates and valleys to maturity.

10. Dreaming to become bigger than Kofi Annan is not enough to make you bigger than Mr Annan. It calls for more. It takes more. Can you pay the price for that dream? Do you even know the price to that aspiration?

11. Search and you would find all the answers. But ask and you would be told only half the story. And if you choose to knock on the door, do so very loudly or come close to breaking the door down; for the Lord has no ear for lukewarm acts.

12. A dreadful world has been thrust upon us. We bow down to the MOST HIGH GOD for strength and grace, so that we can defeat this evil-force leading humanity astray; so that, we can protect the children under our care; so that, we can lead them to the destination. We pray for strength. We cry for grace. We groan for our minds to mature to hold the power that needs to be harnessed for the overall.

13. The Teacher's reward is his pain and joy;
13.1. The Teacher goes to the depths, to the point of tears to receive. Then he is told, "Do not teach it all."
13.2. Out of love and duty, he painfully holds on to much of the knowledge because it is the right thing to do for the sake of education,
13.3. Giving it out piece by piece as students come of age;
13.4. All through watching the students battle with questions in frustration.
13.5. The cane he does not spare. He rebukes, he cherishes,

13.6. Yes, the teacher teaches patience, love, humility, God, life and pain and happiness.

13.7. In time the students leave under his wing for the world he was preparing them for;

13.8. He watches them down the path of life with its perilous points, knowing that many would not make it, yet he cannot intervene until they come to him.

13.9. In pain he watches;

13.10. In tears he gasps as Knowledge's journey takes her toll, because Knowledge would not open the door to the path of Wisdom and Survival until she has seen the students through to the end of her curriculum.

13.11. Nor would Wisdom open her gates to you if Knowledge has not recommended any student to her.

13.12. Ananse says, "The watch is the greatest pain of the Teacher."

13.13. Yet he must watch the falls, the slaughter, the pains and failure of his students, knowing that, watching is all he could do at that hour. After all, it is also a learning curve for the Teacher.

13.14. The Teacher's joy knows no bounds when at sunset, he sits under the shade and sees his students educated, fed, and living briskly and happily. He was a part of their education.

13.15. "I am a Teacher", he shouts proudly.

13.16. This joy is his honour and reward. A reward no one can take from him or deny him. Not even death, because he has seen, touched and tasted his fruits.

13.17. It is a reward for his ascension and a key to his second journey.

14. Divine Plan:

14.1. It is time for anarchy

14.2. It is time for assassinations;

14.3. It is time for murder and bloodshed;

14.4. It is time for slaughter.

14.5. It is time for hunger and anxiety because the time for the hunt is just around the corner.

14.6. Whether you call it rebirth or growth or time of evolution, it is part of a Divine plan.

15. What do you do when you are lost for words? To show the whole world that you have been emptied? No, smile it off and take in a deep breath of air; for in that air lays wisdom and energy that would bring you back to life.

16. There comes a time when you have to pause and recharge your batteries. It is not always right to be moving forward.

17. I am getting late. They are all going forward and I have not started. Be patient. Your time would come. Ananse says: "Commit your ways in the safe hands of patience and wisdom, for the eyes of the universe is watching to take action in your favour as the Most High God has ordered long before Time."

18. No President or an elected officer for that matter knows how he was elected and the price that was paid. Only the kingmakers do, so allow them space to act in the common interest.

19. It is all you. You are the only person who holds the key to your dreams and future.

20. Humanity's problems and troubles are Man-made. The earth's problems are from the species which have interests on it.

21. Africa's problem is Africans'. It is all about us. It all stems from Africans accepting and nourishing seeds of poverty and delusions. But if we refuse to accept the false narratives, if we shall assure ourselves of our great potential and how great we can become, then Africa shall rise. If we shall refute the false world history and low-mindedness, then we shall overcome and be who we must be. It is all about Africans solving Africa's challenges and building our cities. Let us know who we are. Then we shall know what we can do and from that knowledge of ourselves, we would gather the strength to build our nations to newer heights of human civilisation.

22. Whole generations of our youth are growing without elders because sometime ago, a system was put in place to remove

all the parents either by poverty, deaths, incarcerations or whatever evolved therefrom. Or as in the worst case, the parents themselves are empty of any constructive values because the system denied them education.

23.  When you have a dream, prepare for it; work hard for it; pay the price and achieve it. Who can tell what dignity is?

24.  For dignity's sake; for pride's sake; for the sake of our people, let us build our communities. Let us fix it. Let us redirect our energies from tearing each other down to building our planet's rivers, forests, lower species and the air. Let us build Africa; let us fix Europe; let us stabilise the United States; let us hold China to the standards and generosity; Let us be who we can be.

25.  If you would seek power, seek the power to change lives and make them better. These are the duties God expects from His children.

26.  Frightening days are not far ahead of us. O the coming cataclysm is on the horizon. We see self-destruction on the horizon. They see it too. Their pain is that, they see it but can do nothing about it. Who can save a people who decide to bring calamity upon themselves?

27.  Think of the moment and the hour. The future belongs to the Wise and Keepers of Time.

28.  Do you know that, they do not know that, you know that, they do not know what you know? So why would you let them know what you know? If you do, with their resources, they would be able to measure you and you would lose a great advantage. By the time you know this, you would know that, it is too late.

29.  The power to change the society and make it better should be the ultimate desires of all who seek power and, with this desire, when the power is acquired, would lead to deeds of greatness.

30.  Time is all.
30.1.  Time counts for nothing;
30.2.  Time is everything.

30.3.  It is everywhere. It is nowhere.

30.4.  It is a concept only the wise can understand or master on their deathbed.

30.5.  Time is the holder of God's decisions

30.6.  It holds them till they are nigh and gives birth to them,

30.7.  Time determines seasons of conception, labour and birth,

30.8.  Time is the only trusted servant of the ELOHIM

30.9.  Has the ELOHIM not elevated Time to His status?

30.10.  Will any affair of man be manifest without the agreement of Time?

30.11.  Would God withhold the Voice of Time and deliver?

30.12.  Know Time; be His servant; be His student and lo your light would never dim.

31.  Someone finds peace in a song; another in food; another in the flesh of a woman; to another in prayers; and to another in war. Who are you to determine how I should find my peace? Is it the voice of God showing a path or your means to power and domination? Is God weak or voiceless that He cannot reach to teach me when I am ready to learn?

32.  Why should your inspiration be my inspiration? Whilst one finds inspiration in nature, another finds it in beauty or the voice of his love; others in music and some in food. Yes, some in sex.

33.  Do not provoke the breadwinner to anger lest you go to bed on an empty stomach.

34.  Only a fool would make the king angry or allow him to miss his lunch.

35.  There is always a higher authority. And even in a circle, there is always a higher circle within (the circle). As Ananse would put it, "There are higher points even on the sketch of a circle."

36.  Give us war...how? Get us an enemy...make him big...the bigger the enemy, the bigger the war...the bigger the profits...Ananse calls them, "Gangsters Gang."

37. You have no idea the valuable lessons you learn from failure. It takes only tomorrow to tell.

38. Does it matter what the world and your enemies or friends call victory? What matters is what you call victory. That victory is the victory, which matters. And I pray it is defined by a transformation within you.

39. An impulsive young man once told me his mother taught him, "Leadership is discipline and sacrifice."

40. The human mind, which controls the human body is funny and makes the body behave funny at times. When you grow to dine with the gods, remember to come down occasionally to dine with the poor mortals beneath. After all, you are mortal. If you stay too long up there, you are likely to lose touch with the mortals whose sweat, voices and faces pushed you up. Remember, "You would definitely come down one day."

41. When you internalise the words of God, it comes to a point and a time when you become one with the word, written or codified, and with that comes a solid foundation. With that foundation you reach out to tap into higher, and strange wisdom often hidden and revealed only to the worthy.

42. Care for the poor. Neither crave for the adulations of children nor the vanities of this temporal life. They are traps and poisons. Look beyond and you would behold the beauty of a higher world, and that should be your guiding light.

43. The voice of a departing Leader sounds thus: "I know I was given a job and I delivered. Whether it is an "A" or a "B" grade, I believe it is for the present as well as the future to judge. That should not be my worry. But let them who would be my judges note that some of the things I did, were for the benefit of the present. For many others, I cheated the present for the benefit of the future."

44. Go beyond belief to the level of Knowing. For when you know, no one can take from you. You are the one with the knowledge. If you believe, you are secured as far as you continue to believe

or your belief systems hold. What happens when the storms and realities of life catch up with you and you are unable to stand throughout? Let your belief which sometimes comes to you by grace, lead you through the painful journey to Knowledge. Pay whatever price the Teacher demands. Knowing is all.

45. Knowledge never ends. When you say: "I have enough, then another breadth opens." Be an eternal student. The day you stop learning is the day you begin to whither and die off.

46. The brain can go as far as eternity if only the holder shall not say, "I am at my end; I have seen enough and learnt enough. It is my time to rest."

47. There is a missing link, which God in his wisdom reveals only to the Worthy. It is the crucible or raw materials for the perfect weapon for all matters and wishes. It is the link between companions, belief and knowledge; belief and faith; knowledge and faith. This is the link which defines who is great and who is the greatest among the luminaries among the great. How does man know, let alone master this missing link? It is about learning, seeking, crawling forward and staying on your feet.

48. It takes time to make friends; it takes time to build bridges; even in movies.

49. Adamu is a hopeless continent. It is statistically insignificant. Yet we cannot speak seven words without mentioning Adamu. What is it that we fear? What is there that scares us to the marrow?

50. Everybody makes a mistake, but be careful not to make a terrible mistake that would hang around your neck for the rest of your life.

51. You can only educate those who are prepared to learn. For fools, if you persist to educate them, you would only find the worst in you.

52. Nothing happens by chance, so be careful what you say about what you hear or see.

53. Everything is scripted; everything is according to a plan; all follows divine laws.

54. Money, your paper lord, as you know it is dead; so prepare for your nightmare.

55. At the end of this world as you know it, only two lords would matter: wisdom and guns. Of these two, choose wisdom for it brings you to the foot of God and only a rare few can have her. For guns, even fools can control it and with it are disasters and chaos.

56. You stupid gamblers, how much would it take to build the schools, houses, provide drinking water and the health houses and even the roads and electricity? May I ask for $1/12^{th}$ of your stolen assets? Why do you continue to look on as the people rise up in arms out of their hunger and desperation? Do you want to risk it all when you can wilfully gift out a twelfth and come out with adulations and honour? The storms have gathered. The masses are at the gates. Prepare for your nightmare if you fail to heed.

57. They tell the world: "We had a fruitful meeting...all would be well." Ananse says, "They are lying to you as well...when they met, they lied to each other...all parties knew they were lying to each other.... they could not afford the truth... either the truth was bigger than them, they were afraid of the truth or they lacked the energy to face the truth. Or they did not have the authority to tell the truth."

58. Look into the eyes of your children and promise them protection, education and food. And be a man to honour the promise.

59. Beauty as a weapon of choice of the flesh;
59.1. A beautiful woman with a gun, how dangerous can a woman be?
59.2. A beautiful woman with a gun and a smile on her face, how deadly can a woman be?

59.3. A beautiful woman with a gun, a smile on her face, and an opportunity, what is impossible to her?

59.4. A beautiful woman with brains, opportunity, and a smile on her face, a gun and a mission is the ultimate weapon.

59.5. O Man, run from her.

59.6. Ananse says, "Make her your ally and there would be peace in your world. If you fail, run as fast and as far away as you can from her."

60. Love is the only vehicle which can lead you through all doors to the very Throne of GOD. No other vehicle can. Love is the only weapon, which overcomes all. No other weapon can.

61. Do not take your liberties for granted. Noble men paid the price to secure it. Many more are paying a great price every minute, every hour and every day to uphold it, so that you would wake up every day, secured, happy and un-raffled to go about your routine.

62. Ananse says he has lost trust in the human nature. He has lost faith in flesh and blood. He has placed a curse on himself if he ever trusts flesh and blood again. He says as he stood on his feet, earnestly worshiping the Most High GOD, a thought entered his mind. A temptation, which even in the house of worship, he could not overcome.

63. Some have sex for class; others for conquest and domination; for others it is for fun or pleasure; but to the wise, it is for healing.

64. Adaptations of the learner. By adaptations they acquired knowledge; by adaptations they built their civilisation; by it they learnt from the Mother of all civilisation; but when they were mid-way, they said it is enough and by brute force, they destroyed the Mother. And now they are trapped because they did not learn how to evolve into the ether. Children with firearms.

65. The elemental energy and art of sex in love,

65.1. Sex is a solemn exercise so do not crowd it; do not rush into it; do not botch the process; do not rush the acts; do not rush the exit.

65.2. Yes, do not be in a hurry to walk out of it after the blur.

65.3. Rest your body and mind and let them adjust to the energies absorbed throughout the therapy, albeit elemental.

65.4. Then you can step up and out of it knowing that you have properly executed the acts.

65.5. Above all, before the acts, prepare your mind for it and ease into it wilfully and happily.

65.6. It is only through this that you can fully benefit from its healing bursts.

65.7. Sex is a path. If you rush it, it would lead to painful shocks; if you end it abruptly, it is equally painful.

65.8. Rise through it respectfully and say goodbye before stepping out.

65.9. In this, mutuality would be honoured and both would part happily.

65.10. Talk freely about it between you.

65.11. Ask about it openly.

65.12. Tell each other how you want it;

65.13. Do it the way she wants it; do it the way he wants it;

65.14. And live in the process happily.

65.15. For all this earthly life, it may be your only moment of un-disturbed pleasure;

65.16. Wealth has its bitter aftertaste,

65.17. So is conquest and prowess.

65.18. So as she rides you home, control your breaths and work your fingers

65.19. Move them up and down and rest them where she wants them most

65.20. So should it be that, as he pushes you home, emit to him the hormones of pleasure so that he would know that, he is on the right path.

65.21. Admire and feast your eyes on her wavy flesh as she rides gently and purposefully. So shall your brute strength calm her in your moments of manhood,

65.22. Let your mind go free of the flesh and leave this world into eternity, where you shall touch the divine foot hill.

65.23. Talk to him. Ease all his fears away. Let him know the movement and eat all the best of it (And so shall he do likewise to her).

65.24. Herein, you would come out healed, reborn and empowered.

65.25. Ananse urges you to sing to each other:

65.25.1. "I am all yours."

65.25.2. " I am here for you."

65.25.3. " I live with you."

65.25.4. "All your life I would be with you."

65.25.5. "I am yours…"

65.25.6. "I would love you to be mine."

65.26. This is your moment. This is your hour of heavenly thunders.

65.27. Savour it, eat it, drink it and show gratitude to Love making.

65.28. Above all, learn it and be a master of it.

66. When peace and love wash over you, nothing else in this world matters. Nothing exists. All worries are gone and it is all bliss. No pain, no fears, no tears. Diseases are healed and the higher self is discovered and embraced. All in consciousness.

67. Be grateful for everything. Be grateful to the one who makes you laugh. It is such a great gift. It must not be taken lightly.

68. Time is supreme;

68.1. It is the divine fluid which all passes through.

68.2. Knowledge is the beholder;

68.3. Wisdom is the doer and interpreter of Time;

68.4. There is time to plan for a war and a time to fight the war.

68.5. There is time to collect the wounded and a time to heal the wounded;

68.6. There is time to collect the dead and a time to give them rest.

68.7. There is time to hold on to the truth; a time to reveal part of the truth and a time to reveal all;

68.8. The knowledgeable would know how to undertake every activity;

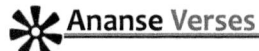 

68.9.  The wise would understand the times and know when to undertake every activity.

68.10.  Here is where the lines are drawn between the knowledgeable and the Wise.

68.11.  The Teacher can only watch the bloody battle towards Separation with apprehension. Knowing the outcome, yet feeling the tolls of each blow.

# Chapter

## 4

*O LORD, let the righteous find rest in you.*
*Let them remain in you even as the claws of this life dig deep to*
*their souls on this perilous journey called earth.*
*Let him who trusts in you find fulfilment.*
*Let him drink from the milk of Mother Earth*
*In abundance and without measure.*

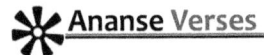

1. The Work which was begun at the beginning continues;
   1.1. The world continues to change.
   1.2. The change, which began at the beginning never ceased; it never ended. It continued; it continues.
   1.3. The fact that you are not feeling it does not mean it is not happening.
   1.4. The fact that you see not Change does not mean it is not happening.
   1.5. The fact that you say it is not happening does not cause it to cease.
   1.6. Heaven and Earth continue to change.
   1.7. One cycle of change is hundred folds of hundreds of human lives.
   1.8. The virgin Mother continues to give birth, shapes her children and ends the lives of some.
   1.9. Man continues to change; evolution continues.
   1.10. The watchers know it;
   1.11. The teachers know it;
   1.12. Let the imitators and the fools continue to claim glory; time would patiently expose them and we shall see what would become of their glory.

2. Regular husbands, super wives;
   2.1. Who are these women? They want holidays in London, Johannesburg, and Abuja.
   2.2. They want to go shopping in Paris, Dubai and Nairobi.
   2.3. They want to live in palaces; they want to drive two cars; they want to dine at the best restaurants and attend parties with the elites.
   2.4. Yet, they want their husbands at home at 5:00pm; they want their husbands to be regular guys!
   2.5. Are they listening to themselves? Have they looked around them?
   2.6. Wives of regular guys do not own three houses; they do not live in palaces; they do not go on holidays in the Bahamas!
   2.7. They drink at the local bars; they live in three bedroom homes; they wait in queues at the airport.

2.8.  Well, seeing their husbands 10 hours a week is the price they pay for the Gucci and Dubai.

2.9.  It is a choice. You choose. You cannot have it both ways, neither can you have the mansions today and say tomorrow that, " I am tired, I want out."

3.  Has religion in the end not brought slavery instead of freedom? Has it not enslaved freethinking and reduced the children to trauma?   What is it about religion now that the world should be proud of?

4.  The power to do good and live a holy life is not buried in religion but in God whose temple is our bodies. The Spirit of God is the only means to holiness and salvation. This spirit is part of man. In His Spirit lies the power and strength to live and overcome, to live a life of dignity and freedom. In this you can mention Liberty's name in the public square because you have known and lived it.

5.  Your life either adds up to -1, 0 or 1. At every conceivable cost, let your life add up to 1…. For in -1 is failure. In "0" is worthless-ness. Ananse says none is bad. Ananse says, "There is value in knowing what your life adds up to. And if you care to climb up to "-1", you have 12 stones to carry; in "0" you have 7 stones to carry and in "1" you have 3 stones to carry."

6.  In pain, in storms and in stress I find God and with Him I see salvation. In comfort, I find pleasure. In the pleasure I find flesh and with it comes death.

7.  To the child, his innocence is his protection; to the wise his wisdom is his protection; to the fool, sometimes his stupidity is his protection. Ananse says of the three, it is best to let your wisdom protect you.

8.  My son, do not take people's love and support for granted. It is only by grace and God's blessings that we are loved.

9.  They say, "When history is written, villains are heroes…" or as some would also say, "Victors write the history and they become

legends." Ananse asks, "What history is that? Is that not the history of poor mortals? What about the chronicles of God? Would villains be heroes in God's Chronicles? Watch your steps and live as the divine laws direct."

10. The mind is all that matters. It purifies the body and poisons it. It sets your horizon and imprisons you. Control it and it sends all the right messages to the universe, and God who watches over all would respond to you accordingly.

11. Pray for better days. Pray that our leaders would honour the sacred creed of their offices. All we are asking for is food, accommodation, drinking water and healthcare. We are not sophisticated yet. We are this simple. This is all that we ask.

12. Yesterday was a good day. Today can also be a good day or worse, so keep an open mind and balance your energies accordingly. Whatever the day turns out to be, go forward.

13. Eons ago, do you know who lived on this planet called Earth? We cannot come close to mentioning them. Or for eons, can you imagine who has continued to live hear? Eons ago do you know the civilisations that once flourished here? We are nothing to them. They see us and brush us off. There are no public words to describe them. Do we even understand this planet in all her worlds? You know nothing. It is time to begin your education.

14. This flesh is not a trusted companion.

14.1.  A time would come when food would lose its taste in your mouth;

14.2.  A time would come, when sex would lose its value and passions would no longer be stirred in you;

14.3.  That time would come when material wealth would count for nothing.

14.4.  In the end, Ananse says, "What would matter is your achievements and peace with your maker."

15.  Ananse says, "Listen to the words of the mad lords;" "a world

of peace would be boring." "A world without war and crime would create unemployment."

16. Do you know the beauty of books? Even if you cannot read its written knowledge, if you hold it in your hands long enough, you would always learn something. Ananse says that; "when all else perishes, knowledge shall be the only weapon which would remain with the ability to lift you up." "Knowledge shall be your only trusted companion and guide." "It is the silver bowl which would guide your steps and keep you safe."

17. Rather think of Love than Heaven. Rather live and walk in love than brood over Heaven all day long. Heaven is a consequence. Love is a requirement to Heaven.

18. By knowledge we build our houses, by knowledge we overcome diseases, by it we achieve. Gain knowledge and apply her to solve your problems. In her application lies wisdom.

19. Knowledge that does not bring relief, solve problems or bring rest is of no use and should be discarded with disdain.

20. The wicked never learn because they are blinded by their wickedness. They keep going on and on till they are consumed by their wickedness.

21. True champions never do anything for pleasure; it is all for glory and the pleasure for the masses. Legends never live in their glories; they keep going for the pleasure of the poor. True Conquerors never do anything for their pleasure; it is for Glory's sake and sometimes in the defence of Honour.

22. What is happier than doing what you love; where money does not matter; where fame does not matter; when all else is dead; when all that matters is doing what you love. This is the ultimate love, which extends your life into eternity.

23. Here on God's Planet, Earth, we reward the wicked and crucify saints. Their good deeds become their traps; their good intentions become their hell.

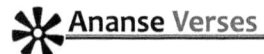 

24. Sometimes the price of success is simply waiting.

25. By knowledge I would plan my life to the end; and by wisdom I would live a life of honour where my deeds shall reflect the majesty of the divine. By the same wisdom, some would live a life glorying evil and the dark elements of this world. In both of these worlds, success does not matter because all would succeed. What matters is the glory and beauty of the success. Whether it was a life well-lived to lift God's children up or a life which left God's children in hunger and anxiety.

26. Eternal Wars,
26.1. You fight to free yourself;
26.2. And in war you preserve that freedom;
26.3. In a far greater war, you protect that freedom
26.4. And in an impossible war, you grow that freedom.

27. When would it be over? When would our children return from the wars afar? Would they ever come home? War and Peace, who says they are different? They are two ends of the same rod.

28. You are a man, not an animal. You know the right thing to do so do it. Why do you expect someone to tell you to do the right thing before you do it? Have you forgotten who you are? Even animals, with time, learn to do what they should do without being told.

29. Listen to that fool, shouting, "sin, sin, sinners would burn in hell." Who has sent you to condemn man? Preach salvation, preach holiness, preach righteousness and lo you would no longer see sinners but holy men.

30. The Oracle of Folly: "Hunt them down...destroy the bold... destroy the best...destroy their future before that future is even born". After your glorious destruction, the future would surely come and you would have no soldiers to defend you. Yes, because you destroyed your engineers, medical doctors, teachers, farmers and philosophers long ago.

31. I met an old man, frail but with a strong voice, and he said to

me, "My son, politicians are the greatest opportunists. They are vile creatures. I am a politician." I told him, "You are unfortunate...and I pity you because the Lord would never forgive your betrayal," He retorted and turned to leave. A distance away, he shouted, *"Do well to deliver the promise and the Lord would forgive your betrayal."*

32. Warfare of our mortal gods. They select the worthless of us and prepare them to waste the best of us. They select the best of us and turn what God has coded in them for good, against the good they were sanctioned for. Ananse cries, "O Lord, rise and save the good, for the world is full of pain and hunger without them."

33. The fasting gurus...comfort is a strange animal;
33.1. There were three paddies, Alo, Alomi and Alomina.
33.2. They were poor and always in need.
33.3. When they had no food for seven days, they fasted for seven days. When they had no food for 3 days, they fasted for 3 days.
33.4. "There would be days" they would assure themselves in their hungry moments.
33.5. Alomi's good days came. He had money and began a life of food and abundance.
33.6. When he was asked about fasting, he said he was spiritually equipped to last for years.
33.7. "Fasting is for the poor, destitute and the insecure."
33.8. "Does the rich fast?" He would ask.
33.9. Alo's good days came.
33.10. And he made sure not to miss any good things he desired.
33.11. When he was asked about fasting; he said there are 79 forms of fasting: mangoes fasting, vegetables fasting, tea fasting, coffee fasting, table-top fasting and many more forms which the Holy Pope has not even thought of.
33.12. "Table-top" fasting is the one for me", he would shout at arrogant friends who dare question his newfound lifestyle.
33.13. Since no one knows what "Table-top" fasting was, he was left alone.

33.14. God is always good.

33.15. Alomina also had wealth and money and started a life of comfort.

33.16. When he was asked about fasting, he responded, "There are many forms of fasting as Alo has preached.

33.17. He would fast when he was spiritually weak.

33.18. For health purposes, he would fast half-day, three times a week if he felt sick.

33.19. For seven years, he had not followed this routine though and no one knows when he would start to.

33.20. Are you fasting because you are poor, destitute or insecure?

33.21. Or you are fasting for spiritual growth?

33.22. There are Alo, Alomi, Alomina and even worse in all of us.

33.23. Hunger, needs and riches have a way of revealing to us who we really are.

33.24. Ananse says, "Fasting is one of the best ways to stay physically and spiritually healthy."

33.25. "Above all remember the values and character which raised you from the dust."

34. The journey of life is fraught with many falls and bruises;

34.1. So count your steps and bid your time;

34.2. What will happen has been decided; what would be done, would be done;

34.3. GOD has apportioned to each one according to how He has made him; and in this, everyone would find fulfilment. Know this, and you would find happiness and harmony; follow someone else's dreams and you would lose your path.

34.4. Know who you are and you would be who you are made to be: a happy and fulfilled soul.

34.5. If you are not pleased with your world, transform yourself into who you want to be.

35. Can you sense it? Can you smell it? It is here already. All were here long before you were born. Show gratitude to the Most High God and your wishes would be honoured.

36. The message of Christ Jesus was freedom and a solid staircase to Heaven.

36.1. The Christ, Jesus, brought a message and path to GOD. Man converted his message into religion; and by that religion the message was lost, and man was enslaved.

36.2. Let us find the Message of Christ and find our freedom.

36.3. You simple man, find salvation and abandon religion.

36.4. By the Message, which comes without by-laws, culture, conventions and constitutions and personalities, we shall be free and find the true path to the Kingdom of GOD.

37. Ananse Verses is not about one verse or two verses. It is about "The Verses." It is about everything and many things outside the book. Everything is linked. Everything happens for a purpose.

38. Some of the verses in this book test your patience, others your knowledge; yet others your wisdom. Every verse of this book is for a reason. Even when you deem it stupid, it is a gold nugget for someone. There lies your first lesson: humility.

39. Everything is good if you would learn to look at it from the right perspective.

40. The Creed of the Abusers, "Starve the people; break them or be merciful and let them know you are prepared to break them and dash them on rocks; at that point, they would accept whatever you give them." "This is our route to another season of perpetuating our power."

41. The god of prosperity is easier to conquer than the God of Salvation because salvation is only for the chosen and leads to eternal thrones of majesty and hallow cities; but for wealth, even pigs could be bestowed.

42. Heroes pass through fires and come out as champions.

43. The Creed of winners: They never give up the fight; they never give up the chase; they never give up hope. That is why they are successful. If they miss the boat at one stop, they never give up. They assure themselves: "We would catch up at the next stop." On and on they chase till they are met.

44. Yes, politicians are the only people in the society who are given so much, but barely give anything back to society and on many occasions get away with it.

45. Every nation willing to be a good Mother must be strong and powerful lest she would watch helplessly as her children are abused and slaughtered by powerful nations.

46. Have you been tempted to the point of your last breadth? Have you come face to face with the human being in you? Be humble and say hallelujah if you have overcome.

47. Every man must know his limits. You must know the limits of your strength beyond which you begin to hurt your soul and body and all around you. Every man must know the limits of his abilities, beyond which he would begin to destroy the very little he has achieved for himself. The wise would learn or hear and take heed; for the fool, if he is told or even restrained, he would rumble on like a bull till he destroys everything.

48. God can vouch for me. He has tested me to the point of death and I have stood firm. How far has He tested you? With tomatoes and hunger? Be humble and pray for His grace all the time even if you foolishly think you are anointed beyond measure. Humility is key. The seal of God is the key and not the foolish adulations of men.

49. Between Love and Peace, and all the values, Love is the greatest but if you ask me to make a choice, I would choose Peace above all of them.

50. Some people usually misconstrue humility for folly. Those who make this mistake are the real fools.

51. If you have been to the North, South, East and West and have not found your solution, look within and find the ladder up to the resting place of God.

52. Tame your tongue and speak words of healing onto yourself. If you do, you would smell gold and kings and princesses would run to your house.

53. Who says wisdom cannot be a trap? When you become so wise that you could solve mysteries, explain issues confounding the masses and solve problems to the level that you are revered, your words become the food for billions and you become invincible. At this point, darkness enters your heart and then you are consumed. Your only salvation would be: sanity, misfortune and pain.

54. Let the arrogant leave me alone. Let them continue shouting: "Sinner...sinner...sinner. I would confess my sins to God and leave my soul to him. Do they know that passing judgment on me is a greater sin? Have they come face to face with those daughters of men in their elements and have overcome them? Have these little men come face to face with pleasure after a lifetime of pain and hunger and survived? Have they come face to face with power, wealth and have survived? Let us all humble ourselves before the Most High; let us pray for grace and strength so that when our moments come, we shall triumph.

55. If you are living with a tyrant, and he becomes unbearable, even if a greater tyrant comes to you with a plan of escape, you would regard him a saviour.

56. Work hard when you are young; give it all out before that universal disease called age catches up with you.

57. If it is a choice between healthy diet and medication, Ananse says that choose healthy diet, it is the divine medicine for all and it leaves no poison within your body.

# Chapter

*"I have suffered...*
*" Yes, you have seen much pain.*
*But have you suffered to the point where pain does not exist?*

1. The world of men is now the world of the Universe;
   1.1. The dominant species is now developed to be indwell by the fullness of the Elohim, yet he is ignorant;
   1.2. As the Elohim turns him, so is evil able to do alike;
   1.3. The visible dominant species of this world is now entities, some vain, empty and dirty.
   1.4. Maybe they were here before us. Maybe not.
   1.5. The world of men is now the world of strange entities.
   1.6. Our world is now conjoining with higher planes.
   1.7. They have made a pact with alien lords and we are food;
   1.8. Our bodies, mere tents to passage around.
   1.9. Our world wanders asunder without course or route;
   1.10. The world of man is without mercy, love and truth;
   1.11. Evil is now here with us,
   1.12. Our world is gone.

2. Every drunkard is a nuisance, a time bomb and a destructive force. Of all of them, the safest is the one drunk with liquor; yet avoid him. The most dangerous drunkard is the one drunk with power. If you get close to him, you are never safe. If you ran far from him, you are not safe either. The most exploitative is the one drunk with her beauty; his wisdom, his talent, whether inherent or acquired. The wise would know what to do with them.

3. Do not hold on to the thoughts of past failures. They would only drag you back. Rather use them as knuckles of wisdom and you shall prosper.

4. Allow time to sweep your worries away and along with them the evils and misplaced resources you were enticed to waste through unbridled materialism.

5. Dream big. Drink deep your dreams. Inhale deep its aroma and hold firmly to the ropes of wisdom, hard work, perseverance and positive thoughts. And when you have done these,

6. Beware of what you dream for. There is always a price to pay.

7. Fight for your freedom. It is better that way. Freedom earned is wisely used, wisely cherished and wildly protected.

8. The wrath of God would befall the wise, the strong and the shepherds if they fail to use their wisdom, strength or their power to plant, build, guide or protect the society.

9. Have the leaders chosen to manipulate, exploit and mislead society? Woe onto them all their days and onto their children if they benefit from the material plunders.

10. Do not be weakened by doubt. Doubt is a poison.

11. God is the guardian of His own laws. Who are those arrogant children claiming to be the custodians of God's laws? He is His own mouthpiece; He is the keeper of his laws; He is the enforcer of His laws. Without human hands He would uphold, grow and establish His laws for the growth, uplifting and salvation of his own.

12. If you are doing the right thing, if you are on the right course and there is no positive results, Ananse says be patient. It is only a matter of Time.

13. Of all the creatures God has put on this planet Earth, the one with the greatest potential is the human species, yet it is the weakest, most wasteful and reckless.

14. Out of Love, I would do whatever seems right, noble and dignified and I pray the love of God nourishes my path.

15. Do not throw your arms up in despair. There are always gold nuggets and valuable lessons in every situation. The graver the situation, the greater the lessons hidden therein. Yes, strive to go past the pain, the shock and the emotions and you would come face to face with a sea of wisdom.

16. Dig deeper, chip off the waste, burn the fats and you would know that, it is true that "your potentials are unlimited." Herein lies wisdom. All lies within you. There is nothing what lies without can do for you which that which is within cannot do a thousand times.

17. You may look without for inspiration but for a lasting inspiration look within. Yes, and for achievement and fulfilment too, look within.

18. Keep it simple; keep it compact and keep it focused.

19. It is always wise to keep an eye out for a setback or a misfortune. When all is going well for you, keep two eyes out for that setback, which can unravel your world.

20.
20.1. Yes, we are gods.
20.2. We are gods as far as we do not satisfy this flesh and its gratifications, nor live by it.
20.3. But can a man, in this age, conquer the flesh on his own?
20.4. Do not the food he eats, the water he drinks and the air he breathes weaken his will and strength to overcome?
20.5. Do they not blind him?
20.6. Do they not produce those hormones, which enslave him to the flesh?
20.7. O masters of anarchy! They raise your appetites and starve you. They raise your hopes and weaken you to the extent that you are unable to pursue those dreams to achieve the hopes. So you are crashed by the vast expanse of the reality and the unattained hope.
20.8. Yes, they are masters of anarchy and destruction.
20.9. Yes, they know how to do mortals in; yes, that architect and his little army.

21. If anyone tells you, "We are now gods", tell him he is a liar. We are still children, babies and infants in comparison with the universes and the knowledge and entities that they hold.

22. Rain, rain, and rain. Rain the burning sulphur;
22.1. The conventional wisdom is that "you do not destroy whole species."
22.2. Yes. But what if a species is reckless, un-teachable, warlike and is systematically destroying other species and thus threatening to unbalance the pillars of life permanently?

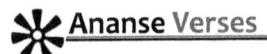 

22.3. Rain the sulphur.

22.4. Destroy that reckless species and restore order, balance and beauty.

22.5. Let them see the rain from afar.

22.6. Let them know that time is up.

22.7. They may tell the masses that it is gold rain. Who cares?

22.8. We shall all know when our flesh begins to melt.

23. It is time for war. It is time for open war. Yes, there comes a time when everything comes into the open. There comes a time when the stubbornness of the fool forces the wise to step out into the open and deal with him. To the fool, he is "exposing" the wise but the wise knows that it is the fool's suicide mission.

24. Moments, bliss and death;

24.1. It only happens once in a cycle.

24.2. That moment when all else meshes into one in a blaze of blood, heat, emotions, and water and vaporises blissfully without limits into the universe's core to behold God's glory,

24.3. (Then if the flesh reigns, in the momentary struggles, we drop back to the earth as stone).

24.4. Yes, that moment of eruption when matter does not exist and all is bliss and One.

24.5. That is freedom. A moment when Man truly experiences that elusive state called freedom;

24.6. Those moments when flesh is immersed, purified and made pure;

24.7. When you do not exist on this plane of matter;

24.8. You are no longer you; your name is no longer Twumasiwaa... nor Asibi...nor Neza;

24.9. You are what you have reached and become; no name, no flesh, no bones.

24.10. You are only what you have become; a force, a part of a force whose reach is unlimited;

24.11. With the ability to tap into the universal existence and be truly free.

24.12. The wise sees enough to remember and climb afterwards;

24.13.    The fool dwells on the momentary bliss of the flesh and wastes a golden opportunity;

24.14.    Herein, we are all reminded to learn to hold and be one with the Universe.

25.    Do not go into an agreement with evil and crafty men. Do not be in bed with them. Neither be in their debt nor in their council. Their thoughts and actions lead to evil and downfall. Even though your interests may be one at a time, it may not be long and they start plotting your fall. Do not take them in confidence because there is no trust in them.

26.    Ananse is worried. Not because he is short of wise words or a topic to instruct on but because of some strange things. Ananse cannot understand why the land that seats the great Roman Catholic Church is the same land that gave birth to or seats the great Mafia. And this one too; "why the two sons of Abraham have decided to bind in a war till death, under the banner of religion?"

27.    Progressive ideas always meet opposition from the status quo. Ananse says, "Before you start shouting change, change...be prepared to size the status quo and ask if you can go through all the way with your little campaign."

28.    Very few people set out to kill the dragon. Often, they set out to kill the rabbit. On their journey, the Universe reveals to them who they are, and they eventually become what they should become. Then the Universe finds a way to equip our saviours to slay those dragons breathing fire over us day and night. But from their birth, the dragons know that a dragon slayer is born. Yes, they know and go on the hunt. But the innocence of these saviours becomes a shield the Most High uses to protect, hide and build till they are ready.

29.    Work hard. Have a good conscience and smile a lot. Learn to say 'thank you'. Imagine succeeding in your exams, business and your endeavours; how beautiful would that be.

30. They say the gods among us go about in sandals; you would not notice them; they are there, they are not there. They are everywhere; they are nowhere.

31. Woe onto you who seek the adulations of men. It is all vanity, fruitlessness, silly toils and unnecessary burden.

32. You fool, why do you say, "The misfortune I am afraid of always befalls me?" "Do you not know that misfortune loves those who think of him?"

33. Of the most important matters of life, you can only learn them through experiences and age. Reading from books only brings a semblance of knowledge. It is not the real knowledge. It is food for children.

34. Free yourself from religion; pursue the virtues of love, truth, humility and contentment and you would truly be free.

35. Young man, Ananse urges that be careful. The world is stranger and bigger than you think it is.

36. There are many worlds. What you know is only one of them. Walk in humility and be a lifelong learner.

37. Freedom has her moments but sometimes, freedom comes from letting it go; at other times, it comes from letting it all go;

38. Sometimes by losing everything, you gain all. Sometimes by gaining all, you lose everything.

39. Ananse says: "Greed has a price which when paid, can be absolved. But when it gets to the point when enough is not enough, then you can only pay the price by losing your soul after which an absolution for your soul shall be impossible. And to that, the LORD asks: "What good is it for someone to gain the whole world, yet forfeit his sour?"

40. Life of the Warrior: "I am overwhelmed by life when I imagine "heaven and bliss" in my life because I am unprepared, but good happens to me if I fight and defeat

evil in my mind." Ananse says; "fight your battles on the higher plane of the mind. If you do, remember to win."

41. Imagination is the right arm of God. It is God's gracious gift to man. Seek it and you would find your path along every situation.

42. Wisdom does not lie in books. It lies in the right application of knowledge towards the achievement of your goals and to the benefit of society. This is the wisdom of God; it serves humanity, protects the weak; provides for the needy; clothes the orphan and feeds the hungry.

43. Children, how sweet it is to be a child. Your innocence is so beautiful. Even when being led to your slaughter, you still laugh and shake the hand of the executioners with smiles.

44. Listen to the wise. Heed their rebukes and your life would improve. A wise man wrote: "Sometimes happiness comes from knowing less." I believed and took his words to heart and I prospered among my elders. In the process, I also learnt the value of patience. When my mother became pregnant by my father, I did not ask how the art of getting pregnant is done. When she brought a child home and said she was my sister, I did not ask how she came out of her womb. I had peace in my mind and she had peace. Today, I know how she got pregnant. I also know how my sister got out of womb.

45. I set out to find wisdom but after several years of learning, I found knowledge; disgruntled, I entered the real world. After numerous failures, painful experiences, tears and pains, lo, I finally found wisdom.

46. Know yourself and be the master of your world; be someone else and be a slave.

47. A man said, "Everywhere I pass, I hear he is a bad person."
47.1. "I cannot see he is the bad person you say he is," I would tell them.
47.2. "Open your eyes and ears," they would retort.

47.3. "I refuse to open my eyes because I am afraid what they are saying is true."

47.4. "If that is so, I would have to let him go but I cannot bring myself to lose him."

47.5. Is it "Love or Folly?"

47.6. Ananse says, "It is Folly but Eno says it may be Love, but definitely something else..."

47.7. A disease, which haunted noble men long before Eno was born. Yes, many a woman has used it to bankrupt noblemen.

47.8. Ananse says, "He who is wise would know what to add and solve this riddle."

47.9. Solve this and you would truly be a wise person, able to guide your life into prosperity and in the process carry many along.

47.10. For knowing and overcoming this human disease is key to greater heights."

48. Freedom is our natural rights as living beings;

48.1. Do not deny any being of his freedom or create a necessary condition for such a fate to beget another being, whether human or otherwise as long as you have not been threatened.

48.2. If someone in chains by your hand hurts you in his attempt for freedom, do not hold it against him or seek vengeance, he was merely finding his balance.

49. When you have few soldiers to fight for you; when you have few friends to fight with you and few sympathetic ears to listen to you, the best way to defend yourself is to fight your own battles.

50. There is an animal in everybody. There is a monster in everybody. You are sane as long as you are able to control the animal in you. You are loved, as long as you are able to keep your monsters from surfacing.

51. One is fighting against inflation. Another is fighting deflation. What is the right balance? The economists know the right balance but would the politicians stop hasty decisions and allow the economists to thrive?

52. The human voice; the human thought; the human being so

great; so strange; so unique to behold, contemplate and look upon. Wonderfully created. His thoughts create worlds; his voices create civilisation. O what a powerful being to exist in this universe!

53. Food should be eaten for the reason for which it exits; to give energy to the muscles. Eating for any other reason besides health is poison to the body. Eating for pleasure; eating for class; eating to please your appetite are all sins! They destroy the natural order of life and threaten the divine balance in the world.

# Chapter

*There is no greater evil than that committed by the government
and leaders of men;
There is no greater misfortune
than that permitted by good men and the masses.*

1. There are different worlds besides what you are taught in the classroom. So be wise and humble. Do not be arrogant and brush about your silly status in your little world lest you expose yourself as ignorant.

2. The Little Children say "The World" can absorb anything and bounce back from chaos to order. They say, "This world can withstand a third and fourth world wars." What if Albert Einstein was wrong and the next World War is fought with nuclear weapons?

3. The MOST HIGH GOD has a thousand laws for harmony. If you break "thou shall not lie", someone would break thou shall not murder" and another shall break "thou shall not commit adultery." This is the cycle eating us up. No one is innocent. We are all guilty of one thing or the other.

4. We break the laws of God from earth to the heavens and as a result create a chaotic and unbearable world. Now when things are out of control then we turn around to question why a loving God could allow such pain and anxiety to exist! Have actions and way of life no consequences? Yes, we broke the laws of love, harmony and survival. If you did not, your fathers did; if your father was as holy as the LORD ALMIGHTY and so committed no crimes, then your Uncle did. We are all liable. We have given birth to a world we conceived and have nurtured her into this monster. If today it has turned on us, let us turn away from the inglorious architects and turn to the GOD of Heaven.

5. The unknown is usually more powerful than the known.

6. There is power behind every throne. So to influence the government, seek that power and make friends; and surely, you would have the ears of the king.

7. It is healing to behold beauty. It can heal diseases and cure mad men. It begets peace and forces the warrior to lay down his weapons.

8. The God of heaven has built some into Einsteins and others into Dangotes.

8.1. By this, He has created a balance to protect the rich from the wise and the wise from the rich and both from themselves.

8.2. If the Wise shall seek wealth he should do so to as far as keep his body and acquire further wisdom.

8.3. If the Wealthy should seek wisdom, he should do so to as far as protect his wealth and know how to do good with his riches.

8.4. It would be an unsustainable burden if the wise would seek wealth to as far as Dangote or Dangote seeks wisdom as far as Einstein.

8.5. If anyone crosses the bridge of contentment into the land of "I want it all", he is surely to be left defenceless and damned.

8.6. All shall sharpen our knives and bring him down, lest we are all doomed.

8.7. But if the Lord of Hosts shall give you wealth and wisdom, as we shall say, makes Dangote and Einstein into one, he surely would make a way to protect you.

9. Every government is a corporation. It has shareholders, preferential or ordinary; investors; and veto power holders.

10. If you find yourself in an uncomfortable situation, do not grumble, do not throw your arms up and do not fold them up. Simply deal with it.

11. The riches of a nation should not be determined by its natural resources, land mass, and or material wealth but the ability of that society to create and support the right environment to help its youth (and citizens) to achieve their dreams.

12. There is no Mother like the African Mother; there is no wise person like the African Abrewa.

13. Keep it simple; keep it specific; know what you want and you can rival the giants and you can fight all battles.

14. Is it true that "Father Markus" is like a cunning teacher? He prepares the lesson notes well, teaches very well but as soon as he leaves the classroom, he does all he could for the students

to fail. If you complain of poor teaching he would bring his teaching notes with all the lessons to the council and you can hardly fault him. Ananse says there is one other thing: "Father Markus" motivates students he likes to pass as a role model whilst condemning the rest to pain.

15. Woe onto you who profit from the blood of men. Woe onto them who profit from pain and anxiety. Woe unto your children, grandchildren and descendants.

16. Why are the pigs so afraid of the chimpanzees? We gave them the spark and slid and they are where they are; they are afraid we shall remember and eventually come to know who we are and rise; and at that hour, we shall slay their puppets and let our light bring further light. Yes, we already know. Let the nightmares begin.

17. Death Cross: Those who loot the public purse do not pay taxes at all; those who earn their living genuinely are dying under the burden of taxes. How did this system come into being? Who created it? Who nourished it? Who is protecting this system?

18. Do not waste your energy commenting on the madness of mad men and semi lunatics. Do not even look at it. Simply move on.

19. The riches of a nation should be determined by the wealth of her citizens; their skills, knowledge, dreams and ambitions. Such a nation is wise, and shall withstand any storm. Surely, a nation whose hopes are on her natural resources surely cannot guarantee a lasting prosperity, because such resources would not last the long march.

20. An opportunity should be embraced rather than be disregarded for ephemeral pleasure associated with youthfulness. If your desire to grasp an opportunity is to gratify your fleshly pleasures, then you are misled. That opportunity would temporarily rest in your arms and permanently, it would slip through them, leaving you sobbing.

21. Let us keep high hopes for Africa, our world and humanity.

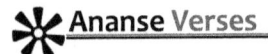 

22. The history of men of honour;

22.1. There is a history that is written and told the world, and another that cannot be written.

22.2. There is a history that we tell our children and buddies by the fireplace.

22.3. And another, which we cannot even bring ourselves to whisper to them.

22.4. There is a history that is so dark that, it is forgotten and cannot be remembered

22.5. And yes, there is another that exists only because the word "history" still exists in our dictionaries.

22.6. Every history has its heroes and villains.

22.7. Yes, but is it the place of one nation to judge the heroes and villains of another?

22.8. Is it the place of one nation to determine who is a hero or villain of another nation's history?

22.9. Surely, and most likely, one nation's heroes are more likely to be another's villains.

23. Ambition is not enough to achieve your dreams. It should be backed by planning and large doses of common sense.

24. The masses hate complexities. They hate the details. They prefer the dotted lines and conclusions. Yes, they prefer the simplified versions. The few who walk through the details to the conclusions become the eyes and ears of the masses.

25. In the perilous journey of life, what matters to the holy throne of heaven is not the adulation of men but how far you went for the good and what you did for the common good.

26. Note that you cannot close your eyes and hope with the aim that when you open your eyes, your dreams would be realised.

27. Ambition is only a driving force, which would come to nothing without adequate skills and character.

28. Acquisition of basic skills is fundamental. It is the key which starts the vehicle for achieving your dreams.

29. Are you looking for the best moment to act? The hour in which you stand is the best hour.

30. Your Dreams are your guide.

31. There is no terrorist but the government of gangsters; there is no terrorist but a bad government.

32. He who holds the pen to the truth but refuses to blow the whistle is a traitor to his trade.
    32.1. Shall the wrath of the nation not be against them as with the looters?
    32.2. Shall they not be held in part as responsible for the pain of the nation?
    32.3. Those who hold the pen and the microphones but go to bed with the oppressors, shall they not be judged swiftly?
    32.4. What nation can survive the day when these special breeds are asleep, coerced or sold their dignity right and power?
    32.5. Write the truth and be damned,
    32.6. Hold the fort and be damned,
    32.7. Your efforts shall save a nation even if you are not saved.

# Chapter

*Two dots could be joined; three dots could be joined;*
*All dots could be joined.*
*It is human regulations and nuances*
*Which make it impossible to join certain dots.*

1. Doubt sets in your story when it is told in plenty of words and as such, it becomes less believable.

2. In times of hopelessness, your dreams console and comfort you, with the promise that a better day would come tomorrow.

3. Greatness has many levels. Some build houses, others build townships; some build nations, others build empires; but the true gods build universes.

4. How could you create a world in the absence of imagination?

5. You, who live in a powerful country or are citizens of her, remember that you are not prosperous because you are wise. Maybe someone was robbed for you; someone was threatened out so that you would have it; someone was blackmailed so that you shall prosper; maybe someone was killed for you. Your comfort and good fortune came at a huge cost to others.

6. Why do I always fail when people succeed? Well, it is because you are always thinking of failure. I hear you worship failure and romanticize her. Why would failure leave you alone? He is comfortable in your house. Think success; think positive and let us see what happens next.

7. Evil men may triumph. Yes, they would but what is the benefit of a decade and two triumphs to beget eternal damnation? Be content with your good deeds.

8. Sometimes you have a bad morning, bad afternoon, a bad evening and a good night; sometimes a good morning, good afternoon and a bad evening and yes, a bad night. Yes, sometimes you have a bad day, a bad week and a bad month...yes, a bad year. Contain the bad moments and work the most out of the good moments, for this is the fate of all who dwell in the flesh.

9. No one who has a stable world would leave his world for yours or come for your primary good. He is in your world, for something: for his own good. Work with him but always watch your back.

10. Fellowship with the saints of God; go to the assembly of holy people and share with God's children.

11. Surround yourself with the best brains. Surround yourself with men who are bold to speak their minds. Among them, let there be only one loyalist.

12. Sometimes your mind freezes when you most need it to be by your side.

13. Free your mind from small things and embrace the greater goals and aspirations of life. There is no greater use of your mind than on these.

14. So set your horizons higher, work harder, acquire the right attitudes and be bold.

15. Believe in yourself and in your dreams. If you do not believe in your dreams, how do you expect someone to?

16. Note that, the society you live in is far more sophisticated than you can understand. It is complex, cruel and unforgiving. It eats up dreams. So be careful.

17. Take time to learn and make regular consultations with elders.

18. Sometimes, some of the challenges you may be facing are self-inflicted and not largely imposed by the environment or someone else.

19. The era of technology and globalization have ushered in cultural changes and have as well, brought dramatic opportunities. Search for these opportunities, utilize them and you would be fine.

20. It is important to redefine your dreams and aspirations from time to time because no environment is permanent. It changes from time to time. As such, create or influence your environment in such a way as to help you to realise your dreams and aspirations. This endeavour, reasonably, should be a collective effort.

21. You need to take hold of opportunities when they present themselves.

22. Do not look down on your brother. Even the fool has his moments of inspiration.

23. Learn to adapt. We are different individuals.

24. What works for Asante may not work for Seidu.

25. You need skills, education, resources, and the necessary challenges oiled by motivation in order to succeed.

26. Dreams would be just dreams if not grounded in common sense and on a solid plan.

27. Note that, sometimes the distance between your dreams and reality could be either a year or a lifetime's journey.

28. Whatever your dreams are, for them to become a reality, it is not solely in your hands. There are seen and unseen hands, solicited and unsolicited opinions and bad mouths, which come to play a part in your dream's quest.

29. Love empowers, so does hatred. The question is which one would you choose? Love brings forth light; freedom and grace the Divine LORD establishes. Hatred brews darkness, anxiety, pain and depravity. It does not ensure comfort nor any form of dignity befitting the glorious being man is.

30. Do not commit your destiny or your success into the hands of other people. Take control over your life and you would never be vulnerable.

31. No person or group can do enough for you. Much depends on you. In the end, it comes down to your decisions and choices.

32. Pursue your dreams and move forward through perseverance and innovation.

33. Learn to network and tap into the experiences of experts and colleagues. There is so much to learn simply by tapping into the right network.

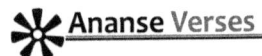

34. Remember that the society is naturally opposed to change.

35. Why leave the destiny of a nation in the hands of children? Have they known pain, hunger, and betrayal? Have they learnt and mastered patience? Do they have empathy? It is too much a task for them. Save them and save us by not giving them the power of state. If they already have such powers, take it back quickly before irreparable harm is done.

36. There is always a status quo in every society and organisation, which is nourished and protected by powerful forces largely invisible. So watch where you step; watch what you say, even your thoughts.

37. The enemy within could be greater than the enemy without. So stay balanced and spread your energies accordingly.

38. Do not be scared by the enormity of what is to be done. Every task could be accomplished with the right planning, level of expertise and amount of energy.

39. Be strong in your resolve and learn to coordinate your activities.

40. Stop blaming others for your failures. People in more dire situations have succeeded.

41. Ladies of the cross. They are God's rod to punish wayward and lustful men. To drain them of their juice and bring moral and financial ruin on them if they refuse to turn away from their sins. These ladies of the cross have no values. They have no mercy. They have the power to use the lust of these men as the chains of slavery dragging them like sheep to slaughter. Their beauty is infectious; their minds know and create every trick to bind for the grave. If you have encountered them and freed yourself, say "Amen" and graciously thank GOD. By their trajectory, their acts would eat off their flesh and bring them to painful sleep. O, how many men would go to an early grave by their hands. They are weapons of war. A war for the soul and dignity of man. The art of sex they have perfected. The art of seduction they

have matured. The art of selection is in their right arm, carefully picking their targets and silently slaughtering them.

42. Who has mustered patience? Who has lived with him and learnt "the art of waiting?" Such a man would receive the best of Mother Earth and his fair share of what the Universe holds for man. Is patience not the last test for the vessels of God? When you have mustered patience, what else would irritate you? Patience is the last hop to maturity. It is the congregation of attitudes and courage to conquer and understand the nebulous art called "waiting".

# Chapter

*I spent years indoors, creating my future;*
*And when I got out of my prison,*
*I started building that future.*
*There was nothing that I was able to build*
*Which I did not build indoors first*

1.   Finally, the end would begin. It is already here;
 1.1.   Sadly in the end, the guns would win and noble men would be enslaved by the ugly creation of our won hands.
 1.2.   Everything would be wired.
 1.3.   Everything would be joined and the machines would be kings.
 1.4.   The creators of the machines would be killed by those who funded them; the creators would sense betrayal and programme the machines to ride as kings once they are gone;
 1.5.   Once they are gone, the financiers who know not how the machines were created would cry, "What have we done?" but it would be too late.
 1.6.   Our experiments would get out of hand and we can no longer continue hiding the truth.
 1.7.   In the end, Hollywood blockbusters would become real, and nightmares and fears would be realities.
 1.8.   Biblical devastations would no longer remain prophesies but realities.
 1.9.   War zones would no longer be on the news. We would be the news.
 1.10.   Our cities would be the war zones; out streets would echo with the clatters of the guns, wails and alarm bells, morning till evening.
 1.11.   In the end, it would all happen and those who longed for that day would live it and dread.
 1.12.   The wise would find his inner kingdom and live in it and in that kingdom, he would flourish till he departs.

2.   What you think you know is a lie;
 2.1.   A time would come, surely, and you would realise it is only a step.
 2.2.   Then you would crawl upward to know more and another time would come and you would know that, that too is another step...
 2.3.   And on and on you would journey.
 2.4.   Be careful of your absoluteness. What you know as the truth is a lie. A huge edifice protected by blood, genocide, massacre and perpetual warfare.

2.5.   What would you do now?

3.   Peace and war are the banners of all seekers. The man who avoids this journey is bound to die, never to be remembered. This is called mortality. This is called growth. This is a journey for makers of history; luminaries whose paths lay the foundations of civilisation, empires and kingdoms.

4.   If excuses are your only excuse for your failure, then you have no excuse at all.

5.   After planning, consultations and reflections, act. Planning forever; consulting forever and eternal reflections are slippery grounds to failure.

6.   The truth of life's struggles is that, rarely does anything come on a silver platter. You must earn what you seek. This is the rule noble men live by.

7.   "Less than 5hrs and it is all over." And so? You are your own timekeeper. You can slow the clock down, keep it still or move it fast. So keep your calm and hold yourself together. All the time you need to change your life is less than 1 second.

8.   Sometimes, challenges never end. They annoy you from start to the end and begin another cycle again. Yet it has tons of gold nuggets of knowledge to beget at every turn.

9.   Call on Jesus; Christos, I call onto you;
  9.1.   He gives without an aftermath of pain, anxiety and regrets. He has paid the price of your dreams and aspirations.
  9.2.   He only requires your surrender to holiness, righteousness and a life of pleasing aroma to the Most High GOD.
  9.3.   Yes, Jesus has paid the price.
  9.4.   Do not call on any other spirit. You would be enslaved for eternity within a galaxy of fear, anxiety and regrets if you do.
  9.5.   Yes, he who calls forth any spirit other than the name of Jesus would be enslaved.
10.   Divine Choice: God created a simple earth and a simple man but man has become too complex for the earth. So, either God

destroys man and creates another simple man or man destroys the earth with all her beauty.

11. There are basic questions to every situation. Never refuse to ask or ignore them.

12. What a world! With a clean conscience I set out to do good but it turned out to be up in evil and the world hated me but I felt no guilt. I set out to do evil but it turned out into good and the world praised me for the good. But that praise brought me no joy. I only felt the tinkering blasts of guilt, ever torturing me.

13. The fact that you have eyes does not mean you should watch everything; the fact that you have ears does not mean you should hear everything; the fact that you have a tongue does not mean you should say everything. The wise would know what to watch, listen and say. With it comes peace and happiness.

14. Be confident in your abilities and attitudes, otherwise you cannot escape the endless spiral of failures.

15. Our children: the children must not suffer as their parents did. If the parents suffered more, the children should suffer less. The children must suffer as far as it is for learning, teaching them the ways of the world, slowing them down or directing them to their paths in life.

16. Education is key to your success so learn forever. Never cease to learn.

17. Remember that you are your best friend and your worst enemy.

18. A leader who listens to too many voices would hear nothing. So is a leader who listens to only one voice bound to be beheaded by his own staff. The wise leader would know what to do.

19. No two persons are the same. You are special and unique. No one is like you on this earth.

20. Do not restrict your dreams to your age. Nor should you allow age to dictate your development.

21. It is important to grow with time, so that you would continue to be useful to yourself and community.

22. Note that, every environment is unique on its own merits. It has different cultures, social values and opportunities. So adapt and you would succeed.

23. Acquire the skills of learning the ways of the society, dealing with elders, cohabitation and survival skills and all else would fall in place.

24. Of oneness, unity and beauty;

24.1. When two people meet, they are two.

24.2. When they move together for a short while, they are still two people.

24.3. When they decide to be together, they have to become one and be one, because it is only oneness and Unity that can ensure their life-long journey.

24.4. So that in the duality of their oneness, they would attain mono-unity;

24.5. So should a husband and wife be. They should become one if they are to remain husband and wife and enjoy the immaculate beauty Unity brings.

25. The LORD is my provider. His provisions are apt and timely in my life. He is never a second late or a minute earlier. I am comforted that He is my provider. In hours of need he is there. Even in hours of denial, he provides me with valuable lessons of life without which I shall take no step forward in life. O if I could cast this flesh aside and desire only the fruits of love, which is enough for me; how happy a man I shall be? Let me kill this man in me. Let me cast out this voice of lust in me, calling for material glory and Lo, I shall be truly happy.

26. Do not be a slave to traditions and cultures, which have no roadmap for the future.

27. Remember that, you are a member of a family, society and a nation and that, your actions reflect them.

28. You need a good character to match your level of education else your society would spite your learning.

29. Influence the society positively instead of allowing the society to influence you into breaking down your values and safety walls. Dare to be different in the society for all the good reasons.

30. Overcoming Evil is necessary for the triumph of Good. Whatever the price, it must be paid; whatever the cost it must be paid. Evil is the enemy of all. Even those who thrive on it are enemies of it. In the end, it would consume them and its stains would remain on the soul of even their descendants.

31. A prayer of intercession and a tale of caution for African leaders and the Leaders of Men.

31.1. O LORD GOD ALMIGHTY, decree and execute.

31.2. O YAHWEH, speak at your Divine Council and send your Archangels to deliver your verdict;

31.3. Speak to the hearing of the Council and let all know that, you do not condone evil nor shed the oppressors and bullies.

31.4. Would YOU let these evil leaders continue to plague your children?

31.5. Would you allow this evil system to continue to exist, O LORD my GOD?

31.6. Have we as a continent and humanity not suffered enough at the hands of these mere mortals and their schemes and petty rumbles?

31.7. From one nation to the other, judge the leaders and pass judgement.

31.8. Spare none of their Council of Lepers;

31.9. Tender no mercy;

31.10. Tender not love;

31.11. At daybreak, send your Angel of pestilence to devour their fortresses;

31.12. Tear down their walls and render them vulnerable.

31.13. Let them know fear and anxiety as your children have suffered under their strength;

31.14. Let them be tortured by tears of early morning;

31.15. Let them know of anguish of pain and desperation;

31.16. Let their joys be tempered with bitterness and anger;

31.17. Let them roll over their beds all night without a single ray of light.

31.18. Let strange diseases plague and eat their bodies;

31.19. Let the worlds see them and say, "These are the men who plagued their nations like cancer."

31.20. O LORD GOD ALMIGHTY, remember the cries of your children and judge them.

31.21. Judge their Wise Counsellors;

31.22. Judge their collaborative Wives who are part of the cancer;

31.23. Judge their Children of age; may they never know peace. May happiness be far from their tents. May all that is ill, be their bedfellows. May misfortune be in their names.

31.24. Judge their Book-Keepers;

31.25. Judge their Mothers;

31.26. Judge their Families;

31.27. Judge anyone who takes part in their rendezvous.

31.28. Judge them ALL...

31.29. Judge the Media which see only one side of the story;

31.30. Judge the Pastors who have tasted their loot and are in bed with them.

31.31. Judge those who call themselves gatekeepers but refuse to listen to your voice or deliver your message. They do not warn; they do not speak your instructions to the leaders; they have become allies and team players.

31.32. Bring swift end on those who call themselves gatekeepers but have gone naked. They clothe themselves with the clothes of material wealth.

31.33. O LORD, have they not sold your children as food to these dinosaurs?

31.34. Judge us all for our roles on the pain of Africa, and humanity.

31.35. O LORD, remember and judge. Is not the Angel of Pestilence roaming?

31.36. And LORD GOD ALMIGHTY, remember them too. Those skins and nations. Speak to the Meteors to crash their temples;

31.37. O LORD GOD ALMIGHTY, have you not said let my people go?

31.38. Remember your children; remember our tears; remember your Promise.

31.39. If they should show remorse and make restitution, O LORD, pause and consider.

31.40. Would you reside in the heavens, drink the adulations of men and do nothing?

31.41. Would you not be swift in your judgement and save O LORD?

31.42. Are these 1% not leading the 99% to dumps?

31.43. Would you not burn the heavens, burn the earth and let it drift afar from his cousins into oblivion but save Man?

31.44. Hold back no longer.

31.45. Thrust forward in grace and in vengeance and deliver all who cry onto you.

31.46. If they shall show remorse and turn away from their ways, from this hour on, then let the laws of old long established apply.

## 32. I am an African

32.1. "Do you know who you are?" Ananse asks. "I am an African" I responded. "Of course you are. I ask again: do you know who you are?"

32.2. "I AM MAN"

32.3. "You are the lover of Mother Earth. You are her protector. You are her child."

32.4. "You are the holder of light. The lover of light and the conqueror of darkness."

32.5. "You are the lover and upholder of truth." "Day and night, through storms and cold breezes, it remains in your firm hands."

32.6. "You are the bearer of all that is noble, dignified and gracious."

32.7. "I say you are the teacher of the sons of God and men." "In you, the children of God acquire knowledge."

32.8. "In you those in darkness find light."

32.9. "You stand for the accused and hold court for the voiceless."

32.10. "O African, are you not the one who clothes the naked, feeds the hungry and shelters the homeless?"

32.11. "You do not run from the needy; you do not see fear in the face of those who assault the sons of God; you do not doubt your duties to man, Mother Earth, and GOD."

32.12. "Are you not the protector & beholder of human dignity?"

32.13. "When all else fall; when the sun sets and the dogs seek the soothing balm of the ashes, you alone remain."

32.14. "As for those ugly scars blinding the world to your beauty and leading you astray, GOD would sweep them to the pit where they came from, for their time is over."

32.15. "Always, remain my child."

33.    Of value, love and skills;

33.1.   Do you want to be valued by your society, be useful to her;

33.2.   You wish to be loved by the people you cherish, be useful to them;

33.3.   You seek to be valued by your employer, be diligent, valuable and resourceful;

33.4.   Do you want to be sought after by your friends and colleagues, be of value to them;

33.5.   It is by services and value that you would be appreciated and valued;

33.6.   Therein the issue of skills come to life. So get it; whatever the cost get skills.

34.   My song for vindication before the LORD GOD;

34.1.   I have not asked for myself more than I need O Lord; bless me.

34.2.   I have not hoarded while all around me go in tears and hunger; honour me;

34.3.   I have not looked at the poor and turned my eyes away, hold me protected O Lord;

34.4.   I have not hurt the animals of Mother Earth O Lord, give me strength to carry on

34.5.   I praise your name O LORD

34.6.   I have accepted your call O LORD

34.7.   I sing your name O LORD

34.8.   Bless me O LORD to carry your name all day

35.   Solution of "The Voice";
35.1.   Let there be a threat
35.2.   Let a real threat be made
35.3.   Let the people make a real threat to the politicians and their anarchists
35.4.   Let a threat be made on their sons and daughters
35.5.   Let a threat be made on their fortresses
35.6.   Let fire and brimstone hang over their comfort
35.7.   Let a real threat be made on their material, wealth and security
35.8.   Let a threat be made on their person and life
35.9.   Let them be told that their deaths would be long and painful;
35.10.  Let them see the fires coming;
35.11.  Let them sense and smell its fumes;
35.12.  And lo, the madness would cease;
35.13.  Roads, hospitals and schools would appear magically and societies would prosper.
35.14.  Let the building start.
35.15.  Dot them in one, two and three places,
35.16.  And we shall, all, behold the great miracle of Africa's rise.
35.17.  Now herein lies the road map if the leaders refuse to bow to the voice of wisdom;
35.18.  List their allies up
35.19.  Locate their residences and put a mark on them
35.20.  Sound the warning and wait for a response…
35.21.  Follow them for a period and then,
35.22.  Then give a deadline…
35.23.  This is not a regime change
35.24.  It shall be a rebirth and growth.

# Chapter

*The end always comes to everyone;*
*Handle your descent with dignity*
*As much as you embraced your ascent gloriously;*
*For that is the way of all men.*
*We reach our heights and fall.*
*What matters most, and not decided by the Most High, is how you*
*descend;*
*Whether in Grace or disgrace.*

1. Anger bestows a man with energies, so does hate, fear and bitterness;
1.1. But these are energies that leave bitter tastes in your mouth and trails of destruction in their wake.
1.2. These energies bring the worst in men.
1.3. They turn that glorious man into an uneven creature hunting down his fellow man like a beast.
1.4. I assure you, the energies bestowed by love, compassion, and honesty are the purest of all energies.
1.5. They leave in their wake soothing breezes binding humanity to eternal host of divinity;
1.6. And bring the best in us, sending a pleasing aroma to the very throne of GOD.
1.7. Of all you do, seek love.
1.8. No matter her faults, embrace her and you would be a happy and fulfilled man.

2. As you know, ½ + ½ = 1; as soon as you hear $Sin^2 ø + Cos^2 ø = 1$ in an ordinary conversation, run because the crier is out to confuse and cheat you.

3. Rebellion is a crime, which should be punishable by death. But what if the rebels are in pursuit of freedom and basic liberties?

4. Why do people blame others for their sins and wickedness? Can a man be asked to do what he does not want to do? Has he no choice in all matters? You are responsible for your actions.

5. The Annals of marriage;
   5.1. Marriage has different colours to different people;
   5.2. Others, because they can "handle" the person;
   5.3. Still others because they have a common interest;
   5.4. Others because it opens the doors to their dreams;
   5.5. Yet to others because the person brings class and wealth;
   5.6. To others it is because it brings honour and acceptance in a society.
   5.7. Few marry for love;
   5.8. To another person, marriage is for peace;

5.9.   Of all, the noblest is marrying for love; the second is marrying for the honour of society.

5.10.  Yet the riskiest, is marrying for love; for the love of MAN, in a world of many colours and kingdoms, has become unreliable;

5.11.  The most profitable is marrying for the doors of opportunity to be opened wide to you.

5.12.  The one who marries for opportunities is the enlightened mind because he knows what he wants and has discerned the route thereto.

5.13.  Yet, he would be far away from happiness.

5.14.  Nor could he be trusted to stay in the marriage once opportunities are attained or a greater door opens.

5.15.  Such a man has a wandering spirit, seeking only to exploit and devour.

5.16.  In his trail lie many broken hearts and bodies.

5.17.  The one who marries because he may control the partner is a manipulator.

5.18.  He does so because he is a weak person and infests the other with the weakness through intimidation.

5.19.  The one who marries for a common interest is the person driven by ambition and has little stocks in love.

5.20.  Such a person also seeks peace, which is seldom found in the world of marriage.

5.21.  In time, their interests may give way to love and harmony if they work together.

5.22.  The person marrying for class and wealth is not to be trusted because class and wealth are fickle.

5.23.  Of all, Ananse says, the wisest person and most practical, is the one who marries for Peace, because peace begets comfort; comfort begets harmony and harmony begets health and long life.

5.24.  For Love is a mirage in these times in the affairs of men.

6.   If you strike a bargain with the wise, however laborious the process or smaller the margin, you are sure that it would come true. Can the fool guarantee your investments even if he says it is for free?

7. What is more fulfilling than a man seeing his family provided for? It breadthes breaths of life over you.

8. Why do you take a risk which, even if successful would bring you no lasting reward but failure which results in an unrecoverable fate?

9. The masses are the pawns in the game of deception. They tell them, "There is no God. Everyone is a God. The human animal has matured..." but once they deceive the masses to follow them, they would turn around and demand, "Worship us, we are your gods."

10. Woe onto them whose gatekeepers are drunkards. Woe onto them who call themselves gatekeepers but keep watch at selected hours. Woe onto the one who says he is a gatekeeper yet accepts bribes to keep his mouth shut. Woe onto the gatekeeper who turns his eyes away from the sins of the leaders and refuses to speak the words of the SOVEREIGN LORD to the nation.

11. Right or wrong, hate institutions. Hate structures, which box you in an iron cage, determining your intellectual and knowledge limits, and eventually your rise and attainments of dreams and purpose in life.

12. It is in the might of heroes, legends and the lights of this world live and set the heights. Failure leaves in them frustrations and lifelong tears.

12.1. O how divine they are in their rise, creating and reaching the impossible to free themselves and all who are bound thereto.

12.2. Yes, it should be said, "They lived."

12.3. Alexander III lived

12.4. Napoléon Bonaparte lived

12.5. Julius Caesar, he lived,

12.6. Albert Einstein, he lived,

12.7. Nelson Mandela, lived,

12.8. Wangari Maathai lived,

12.9. Lee Kuan Yew too lived,

12.10. Kwame Nkrumah lived,

12.11. Ananse says, "O how beautiful it would be to live, to conquer, to achieve, and be fulfilled.

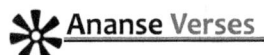 

12.12. Would it not be glorious to say: "I have fought a good fight...?" as the Apostle says?

12.13. Age does not matter.

12.14. So would time and the sun.

12.15. All that would be to you is the glorious world you have created and the fulfilment of the life you have lived.

12.16. Alexander, Napoleon, Caesar and ALL lived.

13. Our Prophets;

13.1. Protect the *"Abrewa"*. Protect the aged and the prophets.

13.2. Feed them, clothe their silky bodies, warm their weak bones, and build them homes to live in and be comfortable.

13.3. Let the society be their home.

13.4. Let them not despise us for a moment for anything.

13.5. Their anger is a tornado of chaos and their discomfort beckons the wrath of God;

13.6. They have no taste in the affairs of the flesh;

13.7. Desire is no longer stirred in them;

13.8. Emotions are distant companions.

13.9. What is left is their voice, the voice of wisdom.

13.10. Their demise leaves our societies dying and our youth grow without guide and wise council.

14. The unveiling is nigh. So is the tipping point reached. The Teacher speaks;

14.1. The name of my church is "The Church Of Light."

14.2. The highest title in the church is "Teacher."

14.3. Anyone who claims any other title is food for the wolves.

14.4. Medicinal sex is allowed.

14.5. Consensual sex is permissible.

14.6. Hypocrisy, when detected, is punishable by a 3-year suspension.

14.7. Sex for sport is punishable by a 31-day fasting and prayers in quarantine.

14.8. Sex of lust, anger, and passion is punishable by 100 lashes. (The act of sex is so holy a ceremony to be disrespected by the excesses of the flesh.)

14.9. Wine as medicine is permissible.

14.10. Medical marijuana is encouraged.

14.11. Any drug for healing of the body is acceptable.

14.12. Singing and dancing are compulsory.

14.13. Music is part of our healing prescriptions.

14.14. Love, is compulsory.

14.15. The love of Peace is a critical admission requirement.

14.16. Filth is grounds for expulsion.

14.17. Anger attracts 7 days of fasting.

14.18. Gluttony attracts 21days of fasting, 71 lashes and public rebuke.

14.19. Pride and his cousins require summary public expulsion.

14.20. Folly is punishable, eternally, by imprisonment until the madness is healed.

14.21. Any child, who attempts to climb a mountain before he could walk, would be thrown into the valley of the lions.

14.22. Parenthood is measured after 18 years. Failure is punishable by expulsion.
(The world is too dangerous a place to add another danger to it or to throw an ill-bred human being into it.)

14.23. Every adult is his own shepherd.

14.24. The Elohim chooses The Teachers and we shall know them without being told.

14.25. Any adult who proves to be incapable of washing his own hands shall be expelled. (If he insists on remaining, any slip would be punishable by 21 lashes.)

14.26. Anyone who sets himself up as superior to another or attempts to, shall be stoned in front of all.

14.27. Slaves are never admitted. If they attempted, they would be stoned till they are healed. After 201 days, they would be expelled permanently.

14.28. It is a Church for free men.

14.29. Anyone who does not find the path after 7days is expelled.

14.30. Our Church premises is the Universal tent

14.31. "God is in us all" is our creed.

14.32. "The path to light lies within you" is our banner.

14.33. "The journey to Light begins with your surrender to holiness, and righteousness."

14.34.  We are all leaders.

14.35.  We are all teachers.

14.36.  We are all gods.

14.37.  We are all children of The Elohim.

15.  War, honour, choice and victory are all choices;

15.1.  We fight a war we know we cannot win yet we fight on.

15.2.  We fight not because we want to but because we have to.

15.3.  We lose loved ones; we lose our societies; we lose our families; we lose freedom, abandon passions and live in hostility, yet we fight on.

15.4.  In the end, our victory is not only what we say it is nor what we make it to be.

15.5.  Our victory lies in the fact that we choose to fight.

# Chapter

*Train yourself to see beyond pretences,
To capture every detail and be able to mesh through good and evil.
For on your journey of life, you would meet them at every turn
and on each occasion, you would have to make a protracted
choice to overcome, lest you would be devoured by the journey,
which surely you must make if you are to be remembered.*

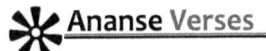 

1.  I am who I make myself to be and not whom you make me out to be.

2.  There goes the fool, so difficult to understand; they claim to know everything but can do nothing. They cannot even tie their own shoelaces! Know your limits and you would be respected.

3.  Woes, and blessings are choices;
    3.1.  Woe unto them who, in the name of God, sell the children to slaughter.
    3.2.  Woe onto them who have been entrusted with so much but have betrayed the trust.
    3.3.  Woe onto them whose voice do not bring salvation but leads men astray.
    3.4.  Woe onto the teachers of the youth who have turned them into food to satisfy their flesh.
    3.5.  Woe onto them, who mislead, enslave, blind and close the door to the face of seekers.
    3.6.  Woe onto those who manipulate the innocent and the young.
    3.7.  Woe onto them who uses emotions to break the young and destroy them.
    3.8.  Woe onto them who only tear down and do not build.
    3.9.  Woe onto them who hold the key of darkness.
    3.10. Blessed are those who teach the children.
    3.11. Blessed are them who guide the youth and feed them on the bread of life.
    3.12. Blessed are those whose words bring freedom.
    3.13. Be blessed, if your tongue points men to light.
    3.14. Be blessed, if you set people free.
    3.15. Blessed are those who feed the poor in mind.
    3.16. Be blessed, if you mend broken spirits.
    3.17. Be blessed, if GOD blesses you.

4.  Is there a human success story without a setback or tragedy or a defining moment of chaos? It seems challenges were created to be our companions on our earthly journey.

5.  Conceive your house on the mountain of hope but build it on the rocks of wise counsel and common sense.

6. Love freedom; be her advocate; but never throw it to children until they are ready for her, lest they trample over her and embarrass her. You would know when the children are ready; they would ask for her; they would fight for her; they would love her; they would be prepared to die for her.

7. O our youth, Ananse says, "You are special to your society. You are the agents for development, social change, economic development and technological innovation."

8. Be a bearer of virtues. Represent all that is good for the society.

9. Love breeds the purest form of unity to the divine. In that unity, there are no regrets, pain, nor tears.

10. Divine decision; would the un-teachable be taught, rebooted or sent on the journey? The nightmare of The Elohim;
10.1. Man is close to the path to knowing it all;
10.2. Man is close to sensing it all;
10.3. Man is close to the edge; that man is untamed;
10.4. Man has strong appetite;
10.5. Man is refusing to look out for his brother
10.6. Would God destroy the un-teachable?
10.7. Should He continue to hold as the un-teachable circle the godly, threatening all?
10.8. Would The Elohim wipe and re-start or rebirth?

11. Be a good wife or a husband and an educator of the youth.

12. Freedom is yours by divine right. So cry for her. In addition, cry for Education; yearn for liberty. Cry for freedom from fear, laziness, and depravity. Yes, it is all about tears, groans, pains and blood.

13. Cry for salvation, and let truth, honesty, hard work, humility and favour set your soul and body free to pursue your dreams to break free from poverty, desperation and anger which seem to encircle you.

14. Lack of opportunity should not be the end; for there is always an opportunity for you to develop yourself. Look for it; knock on doors and break down walls.

15. The tale of two Messiahs;
    15.1. One came with the message of God to show the true path to salvation and freedom.
    15.2. He went about teaching, healing and inspiring like a lamb, among the wicked, without adequate protection.
    15.3. He was stabbed and murdered.
    15.4. His work unfinished.
    15.5. His flock scattered.
    15.6. The enemy triumphed.
    15.7. God Himself had to step in to finish the work.
    15.8. The other Messiah, like the earlier Messiah, came with message of truth and salvation.
    15.9. From day one he created an army. Or militarised his followers. With one arm on his sword, he preached his message.
    15.10. He lived to an old age seeing his disciples flourish to the ends of the world.
    15.11. Ananse says that, "In a wicked world, among wicked and evil men, no precaution is too extreme."

16. O MAN, it is your solemn duty to protect the Minerals of Mother Earth, protect the Trees, and Love her Animals wherein we are all of one chain begetting and making us who we are;
    16.1. How stupid has the man become that at sunrise he mines the minerals for pleasure and greed.
    16.2. At noon he fells the tress for spite,
    16.3. And at sunset, he slaughters the animals for pleasure.
    16.4. Our end is in sight O MAN.
    16.5. From dawn we shall behold the angel of death
    16.6. And he shall wipe till we are no more.
    16.7. Did God ever see us growing into this evil?
    16.8. O yes He did and yes He looked on because power to choose and grace abounds.

17. Would THE LORD GOD ALMIGHTY banish Satan for our sins?

17.1. Who are those calling their evil deeds on Satan?

17.2. Is he the doer of their evils?

17.3. Is he the decider of their actions?

17.4. Is he the holder of the key to their thoughts?

17.5. Has GOD not said He would judge each one according to our deeds?

17.6. If Satan were the doer of all evils, why would GOD judge you for your deeds?

17.7. There is daybreak, hear and wake up.

17.8. Are not your sins and evil thoughts coming from your ego and emotions?

17.9. You are called MAN so you are responsible for your thoughts.

17.10. Is not the Spirit of GOD roaming freely to give you power over all Hosts if you surrender and call?

17.11. The next time you sin, or begin to, remember you are responsible for your sins.

17.12. And would be judged accordingly

17.13. So would Satan, your spiritual scapegoat, for his sins and not for yours.

18. The Misfortune of the righteous is a blessing. Call it the pause of God.

19. What we call evil, terrorism and the likes of them exist for nothing and on their own? Were they not conceived, created and nourished? Are not the actors and players of them educated, financed and protected? Nothing exists for nothing; nothing grows for no reason nor grows out of nothing. Finding the creators, providers and protectors of the system, should be the goal of all reformers.

20. Set the children free. Let them be who the LORD GOD has created them to be. Let them fly to the ends of the world freely without barriers and chains. Would the God of Heaven look on their incarceration forever?

21. The voice of the truly free man is flawless, painless and eternal;

21.1. You may take all my material wealth; the houses, lands, the gold and the bonds.

21.2. Know ye messengers of my adversaries.

21.3. There is something you would never take from me; "my honour, dignity and soul."

21.4. These I forever hold. From these I rise again and roam with the gods.

21.5. What is paper currency?

21.6. Is it not vanity?

21.7. O you who thought I was done?

21.8. All your ranting, barks and roars were but a scratch on the surface.

21.9. They are the first lines of lunacy.

21.10. I remain.

21.11. Yes, I have survived.

21.12. Immortality runs through my vein.

21.13. I hold a cell of eternity.

21.14. I am a holy temple.

21.15. The worshippers of this temple forever protect me as they have watched over my kind since the beginning of time.

21.16. I am a god.

21.17. I live forever.

# Chapter

*Hear the voice of peace and yield,*
*Hear the tales of glory from the mouth of Him who lived it,*
*And be satisfied with the promise of The MOST HIGH GOD.*
*That, true freedom exists and it is available to all men;*
*It is a freedom which neither hunger, anxiety,*
*torture nor death can overcome.*

1. The Man of today, if he is willing and opens up, can directly receive the true message of God unfiltered by false religion and or human structures and institutions. If he truly reckons that he has been fed on false doctrines, the true message of God would make him anew and synthesise his whole being into the true being he was created to be. God speaks directly to you. The voice of "Sampa" is only a medium.

2. Ambition could be a trap. It could easily be a suicide pill. So be careful what you wish for. In all matters, know your skills and resources and limits.

3. Much of the African Elite is the canker and cancer, spewing out rot and poison, which is destroying our beautiful Mother. They have been doing that since the day they were born. Mother Africa gave them name, colour and genes but many have become her greatest adversaries.

4. The journey towards the acquisition of knowledge should neither be determined by the abundance of opportunities nor the lack of it. You are the only permanent determinant.

5. Recognition of your place and role in the society is key to finding your call and identity in the society. And if you are wise, your place on God's planet;
   5.1. A wise hand would script your life.
   5.2. Wiser hands would guide you and divinity shall be your emblems.
   5.3. Hear the voice of God;
   5.4. Hear the voice of enlightened men;
   5.5. Hear your own voice; search for the centres;
   5.6. Draw the line through them;
   5.7. But start from the voice of God and end therein.
   5.8. Here, we all seek for the centres and lines.
   5.9. Ananse is told, "seek the lines and trace back to the centres and from thence, draw thy lines."
   5.10. This is an eternity of work, which no man of our present genes shall contain nor complete.

5.11. Wherein we PRAY.

5.12. For as fragile as we are, we need help.

5.13. We need the finger of God to touch us;

5.14. We need the currents of Him to build and flow around us.

5.15. We need a single drop to aid and empower for our journey.

5.16. He, who would boast, let him say, "I have known the centres. I have known the lines and joined them."

5.17. Ananse says, "Only the humble can say this and the wise does not boast, nor crave for the vanities of adulations of man and mortality."

6. If you lack the skills to achieve your goals, do not lament or chew frustration. Retrain yourself to acquire the needed skills.

7. Every society needs her youth to be active in her affairs. Any society, which ignores her youth in her affairs, is bound to die young.

8. Give a noble hand in building a society that is able to make smooth progressive movements towards new levels without distorting its existing structures. In such a society, everyone has a hope of a prosperous future.

9. In humility, use your acquired and frontier knowledge to break age-old inhibitive cultures and attitudes, which are holding the society back. In this, you would find unlimited reach and endless horizon.

10. Act now. The time for talking is over. Do not wait for the ideal condition. There could never be an ideal situation. There are always challenges to overcome and responsibilities to honour. This is the best time to act.

11. The nation needs your energies, diversities, enthusiasm and knowledge to preserve her as well as bring in new knowledge to move her forward and not to tear her apart through greed and folly. Beware, African Elite.

12. The right Education is a personal gain and a blessing to the nation. Without it, you cannot be an active participant in the affairs of the society even if you so wish to.

13. Create a Job for yourself and stop whining. Do not cry or blame someone forever.

14. The youth is the right workforce, which operates various fields of endeavour by virtue of their energy and enthusiasm.

15. Elders, encourage the youth to use their capacities to create wealth and value for the society. They are an immeasurable wealth. Their output is the source of wealth able to sustain the society beyond ages.

16. Remember that you are required to Pay Taxes on all earnings. Non-payment of taxes is a form of robbery to the state. But in the land of Gutters where much of our taxes go to thieves, it is better paying your taxes to the poor directly.

17. Be honest and truthful to yourself, your society, your nation and above all, Mother Africa.

18. Avoid the lure of money and material wealth because they tend to corrupt your body and enslave your soul.

19. Respect the values of your society and be a good student of them. Respect the elderly, respect life, be humble, be generous and work hard and above all love peace.

20. Why do you count what the youth does to survive against him? Count it as part of his growth process. If he refuses counsel or refuses to sit down to learn, then count him as part of those being pruned.

21. If sending your business public is your way of sharing God's wealth to you among the masses, then may Mother Earth continue to give you her milk to your eleventh generation and beyond. Any other thing beyond this is vanity.

22. You are a cultural agent. Cultural marketing is as much a worthy national duty as your involvement in social work in your respective communities. There is so much in our culture to be proud of and so much as to market to the world.

23. Do not just give birth to a child because you got excited or wanted fun. You must bring up the child in the wisdom and fear of God, the God of Heaven.

24. Learn to follow the steps of great statesmen, and become leaders in the various endeavours of the society.

25. Be not only a peacemaker but also an enforcer of it.

26. Addiction? So enticing and deadly. Simply run. Run from it and from all those connected with it.

27. Do not sell your family; do not sell your nation. Do not sell yourself for anything on this earth. You are far more valuable than that.

28. Do not kill an ant; do not kill a snake; do not take a life unless it is for food. Any act contrary, you are in the debt of the Elohim and He would exact.

29. Today black, yellow or white does not matter any longer, of course, except to manipulators and children. What matters is our humanity. And we are one. We are who we truly are and not the colour of our skin or eyes. Nor the language we speak. Why should this tent, which we have borrowed to aid our passage on earth, divide us and continue to reduce us to babies for so long?

30. If I were God, I would declare any food that poisons the body as a sin. So shall I declare all thoughts against one's self, his brother or sister, a plant or an animal as sin. And it shall come to pass that any act against the water bodies, animals or trees shall be equally regarded as sin. So that, the species roaming the planet as man, destroying all her beauty shall know that, he is being watched and shall be held accountable for all actions.

31. Flow with and dwell within the divine vehicles of love, peace, and harmony and behold the Bliss. Hold them and be free. Avoid material falsehoods and see the true world where you belong.

32. He that is called Man, powerful with resources bestowed to lift, abandoned me. I moaned, groaned and cursed.

Then I lifted my head up, looked within me, found the stairs to heaven and I was reborn into freedom and place of honour.

33. Anytime man disappoints you, take it as an opportunity to draw closer to God.

# Chapter

*There is a land called love;*
*there is a land called honesty;*
*there is a land called hope;*
*Live in these lands and you would be*
*In the Council of God*

1. Infiniteness died on the day man gained consciousness. There is a beginning and an end except for Him who lives forever.

2. You know the right path but you have decided to abandon it and follow the path of vanity. There would be consequences. Do not shout, "Mercy" when the consequences roll out.

3. Faith is inexhaustible but human energy is. Why do you ask me to believe in something human intellect can conceive and create? Is it not a fatal waste of resources? Use your faith to achieve the impossible. The human intellect is equipped to achieve any material wish man so conceived. Faith is used for the miraculous.

4. You are an agent of change and innovation so use your skills accordingly.

5. The African you have come to know as greedy, wasteful and heartless politicians and professionals are the Western educated or influenced and tainted hoards. The masses of our people who have been fed from the fruits of our golden soils are the noblest souls you would ever find. They are modest, humble and wise and above all, love their continent.

6. I have seen God. I have heard His voice. It is the voice of a father;
    6.1. What is that you see, know or possess on this planet that makes you happy?
    6.2. Can you count one, two, or three things which make you happy?
    6.3. Remember GOD;
    6.4. Remember His magnificent power in your hour of rest;
    6.5. Be in reverence of the Limitless power of God, his statutes, and love.
    6.6. As you do, eat to your fill of His abundance,
    6.7. As you revel in His graces, remember the poor and your brother, and sister;
    6.8. Truly, you would be a happy person and GOD will call you my son and daughter.
    6.9. Your body would not weigh you down with worries and needless wealth if you stay in His love.

6.10. On this earthly journey, all that matters is to live a life without hatred, strife and greed.

6.11. By this life, you would fear God and be a protector of His children.

7. Whatever this society has given or is giving to you, be prepared to give much back to her. The good you give to the society would come back to you in many folds. The evil you give to the society would come back at you in the form of a merciless monster with seven heads to eat you up in a long gruelling episode.

8. In the hour of your awakening, you would come to bear that all that matters is the power to reach and take. At that hour, you would know that all that has to be done has been beautifully honoured. Ananse says, "Pay the price for that hour and you would be the man you see within you."

9. Beware all you who live in a false civilisation built on lies. Truth would prevail and you would sink into the caves you came from. Yes, before you do, you shall behold untold anxiety and nightmares words could not add flesh to. The Elohim are watching. They hold the clock of time in their hands.

10. It is your absolute duty to dream and dream big. Your single dream could be the awakening the nation has been waiting for. So dream big and work for it.

11. It is your responsibility to dream to be successful in life and to have drive and purpose in life. Ananse speaks to all that can hear him.

12. The Alchemists:
We never died. We never even thought of dying. We are the Alchemists. We simply changed our clothes and stepped up. We turn $1,000,000.00 into a $100,000,000.00 and so on; we create the billions and from there we build empires and kingdoms. Are we alone? No. Our formulae include the media, the men of power and above all, the government. In our acts, we merely transform money into different perceptions of power and creativity. Our minds, long ago, overcame the material traps and escaped into

the realms where all was possible. We understood time; we mastered patience and calmed the flesh. We are always a danger to society, humanity and ourselves. Moderation is our lifeblood and saviour. Greed is our poison.

13. If you meet those who have perfected their flesh for this world, tell them they are food for the wolves; they are items of experiment; they have missed their place in the council of GOD; they are pawns in the game of learning. Their flesh would not last after the last breadth has departed. And soon they would be discarded for the next batch of flesh.

14. Shining stars, you forever glow in our hearts;
   14.1.   Through your sacrifices we are here and remain proudly;
   14.2.   Through your pain we reach new heights and aspire for more.
   14.3.   You knew loneliness and her fangs and suffered so that, you would understand and educate us to survive;
   14.4.   Because of you, humanity continues to dream;
   14.5.   You created homes and built roads;
   14.6.   You discovered medicines and healed our diseases;
   14.7.   You are our shields and armour;
   14.8.   You uphold beauty and your wisdom flow to all.
   14.9.   We bless your names;
   14.10.  We cherish your memories;
   14.11.  You remain;
   14.12.  Your faults we shall forgive;
   14.13.  Let the children talk their tongues out,
   14.14.  You are our Stars.

15.  Strange Mothers;
   15.1.   Anarchy giving birth to order;
   15.2.   Dictatorship giving birth and grooming democracy in a blaze of fire and water;
   15.3.   War giving birth to peace in a hail of noise, blood and pain in a womb of creation;
   15.4.   Darkness begetting light in the trail of life particles;
   15.5.   Anxiety begetting poise and security from a womb of nausea and trepidations;

15.6. Bitterness giving birth to suspicion and therewith nurturing it into trust and harmony after much destruction and waste. All dripping out battle after battle. Herein lies the necessary strife, which every man seeking liberty must fight to free himself. Lest failure, he forever remains, cycle after cycle.

15.7. Pain, moans and groans in an ever eternal battle giving birth to worlds, pleasure and bliss.

16. When I look into the mirror, I am proud of what I see.

17. The road to God lies within. The stairs to heaven lies within and all eternity is. That which is without is only the false pretenders, helpers and mediums.

18. They are at it again. Agents of anarchy and chaos. They are creating another war. To them it is just another game; another means of control.

19. The Old and the New hold no peace for man;

19.1. The world order of today is cruel, harsh and in the words of the religious, "evil".

19.2. The New Order would not be less evil.

19.3. It would more treacherous than words can describe.

19.4. It is being created.

19.5. It would present itself as new to deceive the masses.

19.6. Lo, it is the same engineers, the same actors, and the same goals.

19.7. Those who know would live.

19.8. You cannot live within it and be yourself or change it.

19.9. To be the person you are working to be, you must create your own world.

19.10. And in that world, you shall truly be independent and truly be happy.

19.11. The Order is not being created for you.

19.12. It is being created against you.

19.13. Are you not a fool to believe it shall exist and grow for your good?

19.14. Do you not deserve what is coming to you because you believed in such an empire?

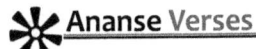 

20. We wear the King's colours. We are his soldiers. We hold his swords. We are a law onto ourselves for the common good. He gave us his seal. Yes his seal is on a paper he gave us. That paper gave us power. That paper deposited a power in our hearts and with that, we move to plunder and soldier because the king lives. Long live the King!

# Chapter

*"It is finished." It is done.*

1. You must be driven by an ambition and a desire to make an imprint on your family, generation and society. You did not get education to just walk through life. There is no reward in dying with your dreams still buried in you. Fortune would not be happy with you. The hosts of heaven would not receive you with open arms.

2. Great nations are defined by the dreams and achievements of their citizens. Their dreams set the parameters of their greatness and their achievements attest to their fulfilment.

3. Without big dreamers and visionaries, it would be difficult for any nation to make giant strides in achievements.

4. Nothing is too difficult for innovation to overcome. It is the conqueror of impossibilities. With him by my side, I fear no obstacle; I fear no mountain; I fear no wall.

5. The only one I fear is myself. I am the most merciless being to myself. I am the most stupid being to myself. I am the only one I fear.

6. I see Mother Earth, so beautiful, young, educated, dignified with poise and composure. She has sat to list the names of her children and to present them with her charges. I saw my name written by her own hand.

7. Mother Ghana, so great. A mother never gives up on her children. Mother Ghana has not given up on her children. Though we have wounded her; although she suffers, she still loves her children. She has seen her future. She believes in it because she is creating it. Fiercely she protects her children from wolves. And soon, tired of the folly, she would take her stand and go to war for her pride and children.

8. Mother Africa calls...let her children respond to her... She is selecting her soldiers for her liberation.

9. You want my files? They are not in the cabinets and drives. They are not even in my head. They are in heaven. I access them when

needed and the password to them is "HAPPINESS". I cannot reach them under duress nor coercion.

10. "The dreams would be achieved. The charge would be honoured." Ananse says, "These are the words and tone of achievers."

11. The natural resources of the nation and favourable geographic factors would serve the nation no purpose towards great achievements if they are not matched and motivated by a great sense of purpose, drive and leadership.

12. Be Your Own Person. Carry your own burden. Be prepared to bear the consequences of your own actions.

13. Neither be a burden to your families, friends nor society.

14. Think critically and use your mental power. Through this power, you shall live to celebrate your success.

15. Do not be afraid to think outside the box, after all the price of doing nothing is worse than the price of attempting and failing; for in the failure of attempting something are great nuggets of lessons but in doing nothing is stagnation and rot.

16. Be prepared to go against popular opinions, conventions and the experts.

17. Neither be a puppet of the status quo nor an advocate of it without analysing it, for the status quo is a product against you and a system good for the creators.

18. Never forget your environment in the time of comfort. It is hostile, ever changing and takes no prisoners.

19. Every society turns hostile at one point or the other. They are uncertain and volatile. How you manage your affairs determines your survival.

20. Do not lose the code: honour, dignity and self-respect.

21. Do not lose the sense of order and procedure. Planning is everything.

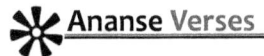 

22. In the absence of heroes to emulate, be your own hero.

23. Be Progressive in your thinking. The environment is never static.

24. Never despise the Counsel of the wise.

25. Educate yourself and find a foothold in life.

26. Do not let politicians tell you what they have for you. You would end up being confused. Tell them what you need from them.

27. There is a lot of wisdom in the sayings of our fathers. Seek them and tie them around your neck.

28. My truth, your truth, our truth; the truth that matters is the truth that brings freedom, salvation and keeps the peace of man and his society.

29. Be suspicious of an environment which neither inspires nor provides a sense of hope for tomorrow. It would kill and destroy you in the most painful of manners. Run from it; do not hold any of her values to your heart, lest you buy into her lie and die off.

30.  Sunset at dawn;

30.1.  Cry for those who lost their youthfulness and its vigour through misfortune, the environment, war or tragedy.

30.2.  Share their pains with them.

30.3.  Listen to their rattling.

30.4.  Watch them with benign eyes.

30.5.  Bemoan them and never hold it against them when they are bitter.

30.6.  They lost something neither words nor banner or any wealth could pay for.

30.7.  Do not deny the youth their days or time at the playground.

30.8.  Let them revel in the flow of their energies and say, "my child, jump around, dance, sing and make merry."

30.9.  Soon, all their energies would depart them.

30.10. Then their minds would be clear of all cobwebs.

30.11. Hold them as far as within the boundary of the growth bowl.

30.12. Lest they commit blunders of lifelong consequences.

# Chapter

*Root yourself in the faith of God....*
*...that He lives and answers the prayers of his children*
*and all who cry onto him...*

1. Powerful people are always a threat to new ideas which seek to undermine the status quo.

2. Do not step on the toes of powerful men. Neither test their anger, kindness nor embarrass them.

3. Do not go into business with short-sighted persons. They are always looking for quick returns. They are impatient. Soon you would be taken over by events and new trends and surely, you would be chased out of business.

4. Do not dine with the greedy, ruthless and selfish people. If you must, do so with a long spoon.

5. Do not make a deal with the devil. His deals always go wrong and you would be the loser.

6. In every society or organisation, there are powers behind the scenes. So tread cautiously.

7. Be humble and respectful to anyone you meet. You may be meeting God or the messengers of Him.

8. Pick the battles which are necessary and not for the fun of it. A battle, which when in victory, does not guarantee freedom and glory is not worth fighting.

9. You will win the Fight.

10. Do not lose hope. Have hope in our human nature. Take strength in your will that, from this depth of rot and vanity, the righteous shall rise to the glorious heights of human purity.

11. The human will when combined with thought and proper actions become a force, which can surmount any obstacle.

12. You should believe and continue to develop your dreams.

13. Have hope in the transformational power of time. Time brings healing. Time strengthens. Time brings change.

14. Storms always pass away no matter how fierce they are.

15. Live your dreams and hold on to them. Time would bring healing, growth and restoration.

16. Remember that, your big dreams may be a threat to someone. So learn to keep your mouth shut.

17. Sacrifice for the future.

18. Do not be worried about the little you have. Concentrate on what you can do with that little. People have built nations and business empires from very little and less.

19. No generation is perfect. So when you sit to accuse earlier generations and pass judgement, remember that, their times were different; their weapons were different, so were their priorities and aspirations. If you fail, one day a ruthless generation would rise to prosecute and put your head under the guillotine.

20. Leave footprints for the future. This would be your legacy to your humanity.

21. You live in minutes, hours, days, weeks, months, and years. I live in seasons, moments and eons. How could our standards be the same? How could our knowledge of this world be the same? I am a god and you are a mortal. Ananse says beware and live in the world The ELOHIM has created for you. Do not aspire for the seat of God in the spirit of arrogance.

22. Fight for an open, accountable and visionary leadership.

23. The society must hold leadership accountable to their promises, actions and negligence. In this matter, ethnicity, colour or ideology should not matter. What should matter is that whether leaders have dispensed their duties in honesty or have looted the state. In dispensing their duties, we all gain whether black or brown, left or right as much as we all lose when they loot for their families and greed.

24. Pursue excellence over mediocrity and contentment over greed. For in virtues lie honour and dignity while you meet bitterness and emptiness in vices.

25. Do not allow deafening noise of the empty barrels to drown your wise counsel. Stay on your feet and let time give you recognition.

26. Do not expect success to be handed over to you on a silver platter. You would be a fool to think or feel that way.

27. Remember, sometimes you have to bang on doors. A soft and polite knock would not suffice.

28. Kings, queens and gods in chains;
 28.1. Rise up, O man, and begin your divine journey.
 28.2. Lift your head up and know that you have been liberated to rise to the throne of God and speak face to face with HIM.
 28.3. Kill the flesh, kill the self; kill the ego and see who you truly are.
 28.4. Know the true God because He is your father. He has given you the right of sons and daughters.
 28.5. O man, O God, we are his fellow creators. A right THE MOST HIGH GOD has granted us.
 28.6. If only we shall awake from our slumber; O how great our stars shall be.

29. Let your maturity show in your actions. Saying "I am matured" is the first sign of immaturity.

30. Hear, O Africa;
 30.1. We must build our youth so that they are able to stand on their feet as men with a unique destiny of lifting a continent.
 30.2. We must tell them who they are;
 30.3. We must teach them to be bold;
 30.4. We must open them up to set their horizons high;
 30.5. We must tell them that, they are the first nation;
 30.6. They should be able to rub shoulders with the American, Chinese and the British and say; "I am a Ghanaian, Nigerian, and Zimbabwean or an Egyptian."
 30.7. They should shout to the world that; "We are African."

31. Seasons come and go but Time is eternally continuous;
 31.1. Time is upon us. That time is here.

31.2. We have just not seen it, when Africa would be synonymous to anything and everything wise, holy, righteous, honour, and wealth.

31.3. It shall be said, "Africa..." and it shall be done.

31.4. The world would say, "Go to Africa" and it shall be.

31.5. But for now, parts Africa is ruled by evil, cowards, and many of her shepherds are greedy, lack vision and basic wisdom.

31.6. This regime shall be defeated and the true clothes of Africa shall be revealed.

31.7. This is the time to take arms not against foreign invaders but our evil rulers.

32. Sometimes self-criticism is good for healing. When done at the right moment, it becomes a self-medication.

33. Learn to laugh at yourself. How much laughter can those haters throw at you when they see you?

34. The pursuit of new goals sometimes requires unconventional means. Quit the comfort zone, and roll up your sleeves.

35. Those of you loved by God should remember to worship and praise Him all day. Bless Him for His care and protection; worship Him for His foresight and unsurpassable wisdom; bless Him for His love. Those loved by the Lord, should worship Him all your lives. This is a small price to pay for His love. Those of you He has willed to put in the firing line all your life, to feed the loved ones from your tears, breadths and trails, should also bless His name. It is a great honour to serve the Lord. The ELOHIM is your strength and shield, protecting, guiding and guarding you till your time is done.

36. Love the woman you call "wife";

36.1. Let her breast be enough for you.

36.2. Let her food be sufficient.

36.3. Let her voice forever ring in your heart so that, your path would be straight and your feet steady.

36.4. For we live in a world of many storms and winds. Even the Master is sometimes shaky.

36.5. Let her thighs keep your blood eternally flowing within your veins and arteries in good health.

36.6. If you grow tired of her looks, change her appearance.

36.7. A small change in her looks could do the impossible to get her lovely again.

36.8. If her food becomes too familiar, ask her to change the cuisine;

36.9. If her thighs grow familiar, let her tan them.

36.10. Love her.

36.11. Never leave her for a fleeting softness of the trained woman who is out to suck your energies to keep her sinking boat afloat.

36.12. The best gift we could give a marriage is love.

36.13. Love is above all, even if it is a treacherous journey.

37. Sometimes we forget not because we are daft. Sometimes we do because we seek to protect life and curtail the needless flow of blood. In certain worlds, a long memory is one of the weakest assets. It is a danger to you.

# Chapter

*Let us protect our rivers,*
*Let us protect our air,*
*Let us protect our forests,*
*Let us build more forests and their ecosystems.*
*Let us protect the land we eat from.*
*They are our primary guardians*

1. Ananse says he has observed keenly, to answer why some bondmen slip. He says, "Some are for pleasure, another is for needs, yet another is for class." Ananse observed also that, "Others are for conquest, another is for momentary love and many more for weakness." Ananse says, "The strangest of all is a bond man crawling on his knees to drip into the house maid. The most rewarding of all was the one for Sanity." The bond embraces peace after the fall even as their conscience puts spanners in their nervous system.

2. Protect your physical body from harm and diseases by practising personal hygiene.

3. Protect your minds and souls from unhelpful foreign cultures and voices by staying true to your dreams, creed and humanity.

4. Young man, protect your mind. This means that sometimes you need guidance as to what to read and watch as well as what you should do with your life and issues worth pursuing in this life.

5. Show great Reverence for Time. You have no idea how much could happen within a second. A universe could be created or destroyed within a second.

6. When a response is too short, it connotes fear and doubt; when it is rather long, it loses traction. The wise response is that which uses the appropriate number of words.

7. Do not turn your back to society because you are part of the human society.

8. In a competitive world, your confidence and outlook is as good as your Bachelor of Science (BSc), Master of Arts (MA), or even Master of Business Administration (MBA).

9. You cannot succeed in life by being like any other person. You have to be unique, confident, bold and competitive.

10. Between fear of making wrong choices and not making a choice at all, take the risk and make a choice. The act of not making a choice is a seal of cowardice.

11. This is the time. This is the hour. As a continent, let us rededicate ourselves to higher consciousness. As species let us pledge ourselves to a higher cause. A cause earlier generations could only dream of. This is the hour.

12. Choices are necessary elements of growth and maturity. But be careful of the type of choices you make. They can make or blur your path. Make choices with your heart, mind and upon lots of counsel.

13. Choices and their consequences are necessary for learning. But pray the consequences of your choices do not follow you for the rest of your life.

14. You claim to know Mother Africa. You do not. The Africa you know is the political Africa; corrupt and lacks direction. You have never known *Cultural Africa*. You have never known our colours, airs, instincts and hearts.

15. Mother Africa is a wounded Mother. Her own children have pierced her heart with betrayals.

16. Rejoice, O children, because Mother Africa lives. She is immortal. She is beyond flesh and blood. She rises with the clouds of the heavens as her clothes and thunder bellows her voice. She fumes at the enemies and withdraws wisdom from them so that they are destroyed by folly and ignorance. As for her children, when the end of their trials shall come, she would lift them up to glory.

17. The world shakes because the Princes and Princesses are awoken.

18. Slay the traitors. Destroy them. They are the temples, which have haunted Mother Africa. For, flesh they seek to betray that which is divine and immortal.

19. The purest of wealth is the possession of love towards all life, right from your body, your society, to the nation, this universe and wherever life is found. Whenever you know and you extend,

you continue to amass wealth, which neither the wish of man nor any human institution can dim. All wealth would pass except that which God has given man to wear and hold for his security and passages.

# Chapter

# 16

*By the laws of men you live and pour out evil against your brother. Why do you now invoke the laws of God: "love, forgiveness, generosity..." when your brother decides to live by the laws of men as well? Why do you hold the wise in contempt, when he says, "You reap what you sow?"*

1. Note that every decision has consequences. So be prepared to bear the consequences of your decisions. The wise would stand and face the music and be done with, but the fool would dance around the music till he is consumed by it in his days of rest and comfort.

2. Of runners, blame kings and deniers;
   2.1. People who run from their problems never solve them. Yes people who deny their problems never find security
   2.2. Stop blaming others; you may be the problem.
   2.3. How long would you continue to say, "It was not my fault...it was this or that or this person or that person?"
   2.4. How long would you continue to blame others?
   2.5. The more you blame others, the more complicated your problems become.
   2.6. The longer it takes for you to come home, the nearer to eternity you are to solving your problems.
   2.7. Be the man you are to be. Take hold of your problems and solve them as a man.
   2.8. Face them in broad daylight and you shall prosper.
   2.9. How long would you continue to run?
   2.10. How long would you continue to hide?
   2.11. This is the time.
   2.12. This is the hour.

3. Quite a number of challenges are as a result of the actions, inactions and choices you make.

4. There comes a time when you would know that good and evil are of one tree. All that makes the difference is the human Will and Choice.

5. Those who deny the people their food should be certain that when survival of the masses is threatened and they tip over, their heads would be the only price to avert the anger of the people.

6. When you go to the house of a wealthy person to ask for favour, ask for one favour at a time. If you ask for more than one, he may have doubts about your intentions and that may hurt you. If you

asked for more than one favour and he chooses to honour only one, thank him generously and go home happily.

7. Beware of free gifts; beware of gifts; be wary of favours.

8. Trading places;
   8.1. Today we do not trust vehicles to drive themselves and keep us safe.
   8.2. Tomorrow, it would be the vehicles and machines, which would not trust humans.
   8.3. The machines can cook better than we do now
   8.4. Their services would be more trusted than human agents
   8.5. Even their sex acts would be more reliable than the human can give each partner, even as their inadequacies would remain.
   8.6. They would be faster, more efficient and trusted
   8.7. They would eat away much of our humanity and make us less beautiful
   8.8. We would become mechanical, less human, and anti-social.
   8.9. Then there would be parity
   8.10. And eventually, they would take over.

9. The nation which would maintain her prosperity and survive the future, is the one with the military and security capabilities to defend her wealth. Without it, a nation is just a fly at the mercy of the powerful to be crashed at will.

10. Of saints, religion, man and freedom;
    10.1. We must crash the false screen religion imposes on the Light of God so that we would force man to live holy and righteous lives.
    10.2. Those who have taken refuge in the false security the offices of religion offers should be exposed
    10.3. And led to the light- the true light which brings freedom here on earth and eternal.
    10.4. Failure, we are all at risk of irreversible damage.
    10.5. Religion should no longer be allowed to be an excuse for filth and carnage in the houses of God.

10.6.   In it, corrupt standards of morality, holiness and sanity have been established.

10.7.   All falsehoods finding refuge.

10.8.   The Human body, the temple of God, should be given its rightful place, as the first of all.

10.9.   The pursuit of her purity, health and harmony with all living habitats should be elevated and blessed.

10.10.  Here we are, living as slaves because we are taught, coached and blinded to see God in buildings defined by human hands and dirt, while we, the Light, crouch in darkness.

10.11.  Have we not harmed ourselves enough?

10.12.  Have we not come to the knowledge of ourselves?

10.13.  Should we not say, "freedom now?"

10.14.  Pull down the temples if they would not talk of the light or allow you to seek the light.

10.15.  Smash the altars if they would not withdraw and allow you to be "the first."

10.16.  They are merely shelters. You are everything.

10.17.  Let's meet in our homes, let us gather under the trees, and sheds;

10.18.  Let us share the light in our offices and buses and lo, Freedom would come. She is here.

10.19.  Pull their monuments of slavery down if they persist in substituting it for your true song of freedom.

10.20.  Smash their faces and expose their nakedness,

10.21.  Let your song of freedom come Home O LORD

10.22.  Let Ananse also say to the world; "today, freedom has come to those held under captivity. Freedom has come to those once lost. On her wings are joy, a home and Hope."

11.  Contain your demons. Do not let them run over you and destroy. You think you are the only one plagued by them? We all are. Even the saints are. Even Dreamers. This is our lot as humanity. Overcoming is part of our growth.

12.  O Dreamers; so bold, so stupid; so naïve. Yet we need them to show the future. Without them we are stunted.

13. The enemy is not ready. It is not big enough yet;

13.1. Why has the first bullet for the third world games not fired?

13.2. The ground is rife, the actors are ready, so are the weapons.

13.3. What is missing?

13.4. There is one key element not in place.

13.5. What could it be?

13.6. May be the enemy is not ready.

13.7. It is not big enough.

13.8. The dragon must be fed, nurtured and set loose willingly.

13.9. It has to be bred to be belligerent, ruthless and "blamable"

13.10. Then the architects would say, "We have to tame the dragon lest it endangers us all."

13.11. And the perpetual benign masses would say, "Let the games begin."

13.12. So now, they are building the alliances.

13.13. They are laying the ground-work, drilling the armies, playing and testing the war games for the Grand Game.

13.14. They are giving the dragon a character;

13.15. They are preparing the plausible narrative for the masses.

13.16. O the beloved and pampered masses.

13.17. Then a full cycle is set in concrete.

13.18. Then fate would take over.

13.19. The architects would not tell what is to come or what is to follow.

13.20. Ananse can only say, "Time would resolve all matters and what is to follow."

14. To be greater than the Master, you must learn beyond the master; to find yourself, you must take risks beyond your current ability; to free yourself, you must go beyond the syllabus.

15. I choose my wars. I choose my end. I choose my path. I see them all. I know them all. What I did not choose is nature of the journey. That is in the wisdom of the ELOHIM. All is set. You choose your end and the path is laid out before you. Bless the SOVEREIGN LORD for the power and gift of choice. The gift was given the day I was born. I am only now able to exercise it because I ceased to be a child and or slave not long ago.

16. The most powerful of us are those whose wealth are invested in debt, favour, mercy, love, humility, integrity, peace, harmony, truth, grace, contentment and the love of rivers, trees and living things.

17. Who has defeated taste? Who has defeated smell? Who has defeated the tickles of the flesh and has mustered the power to look into what is real and touched and consumed it? He is the only true free person. He is the only true student who can rise to the highest levels of knowledge.

18. They speak and you see light and with that light, happiness is born in your hearts to energise you to higher grounds and on your journey. They speak and you see clearly to walk in the light on your journey. Do you know the pains and torments they crawled through to give birth to your dreams? Have you considered the price paid? They lost happiness to make way for your happiness; they lost peace to acquire your drive; they cried so that you may laugh. They walked in darkness so that you may learn to understand light. They suffered for us to know the path. They lost themselves for your sake. Now, do you have the right to question them, when they create their own rules and live by them? Do you have the right to question them when they create their own world and live in it? Ananse advises, "All that should matter to you is to live your life; fear God, obey His laws, love your neighbour, brothers and sisters and be dedicated to your duties. The rest belongs to The MOST HIGH GOD. If you would harbour feelings for them, it should be pity, sorrow and pain. They chose a life of pain for all our sake. They are called Eagles and Pathfinders.

19. The B.I.B.L.E is the only sure way to the throne of God in eternity. But to make the journey to eternity, the Bible is not enough. The path to the knowledge and wisdom leading to the eternal rest lies in manifold books. Some open. Others free. Many hidden. Some untold. If any man shall tell you the understanding of the Bible lies only in the B.I.B.L.E ask him to show you his closets. Seek love and knowledge. Seek wisdom. Follow the masters. Read their lips, eat their words, hang on

to their knowledge and lo, the B.I.B.L.E shall be one with your bones and soul. Then, you would make your way straight home, where darkness shall neither preside nor reside.

# Chapter

*Burn the fats; never stop till you reach your goals*

1.   All virtues are selfish, greedy, uncompromising and errant;
1.1.   They only know themselves and none other
1.2.   It is either alone or no other;
1.3.   "Love is the eldest of my children," Wisdom says.
1.4.   But if you shall miss a mark and step into the house of Affection, and call her "Love", Affection would caution you, "I am Affection" and Love would thus caution Affection, "You are not me."
1.5.   If you pass by Peace and call him "Harmony", he would caution, "I am not Harmony" and Harmony would also respond in kind.
1.6.   So would 'Generosity" warn you if you miss him for "Kindness."
1.7.   On and on they would fight, erecting walls of iron till they forget each other and tear their common thread into pieces
1.8.   Lo, on your journey to the house of "bitterness", if you miss a step and step into the house of "Anger", he would give you a seat, smile to you, show you his bombardments and points you the way to the house of Bitterness with the words, "my brother Bitterness is more romantic than I am. Never stop anywhere till you reach him."
1.9.   And so Vices look out for each other;
1.10.   They hold court for each other,
1.11.   They defend and encourage each other,
1.12.   So they have become a far more potent family, able to take nations on whole and show off their bombardments.
1.13.   Shall we not remember that, "There is strength in unity?"
1.14.   Shall we not learn that together we are stronger even if we are on a course against God?
1.15.   Would Virtue learn and bring healing to the world of men and animals and our plants?
1.16.   Who is Virtue if she would not learn and persist to hold Vice from continuing to triumph?
1.17.   Shall we say, Virtue should learn from the Bond of Vice?
1.18.   And in the lands of egoistic little men, would Virtue find the right stocks to thrive on and ride to conquer?
1.19.   Hear and shout it upon the Malls, market places, on the streets and the stadia, "come together and let's gather for

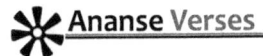
unity and for Love."

1.20. Love without support is like a shadow on the wall. No matter how sharp it is, you cannot hold it in your arms.

2. It is time to stand up and be noticed. You have been in the shadows for far too long.

3. You have been running for a long time. Stop running. Say, "I am no longer a runner. I am no longer a slave."

4. Do not be enticed by empty adulations, financial conveyances, perks and empty luxury. Your soul is immortal in the realms of mortality. Hold it for Truth and in defence of it.

5. Stay true to your ideals and principles at all times. You are the master. You are the decider.

6. Unity is stronger than any outside force.

7. In a lifetime of luxury, I have lost touch with the reality of my world. How can I serve my people? How can I be their leader? How can I provide for them when I do not understand them?

8. Knowing, overcoming and developing is key to a man's growth;
   8.1. The man who does not know himself is lost.
   8.2. A man should know his strengths and weaknesses.
   8.3. A man should build on his strengths;
   8.4. He should overcome his weaknesses;
   8.5. A man who does not know who he is, is bound to falter in many aspects of his life.

9. To the glutton, food is a poison to his body and soul; but to the hungry, food is medicine to his body and mind.

10. What makes music? Is it the lyrics, the voice, the emotions it stirs in us, or the instruments accompanying it? Or is the human designation that certain rhythms accompanying the human voice in a typical sound is called "Music?"

11. If you look at the smaller issues, you would miss the big picture. If you look at the big picture for far too long, you would miss

the smaller issues necessary to support the attainment of the big issues. The wise would know what to do. But Ananse would offer advice thus; "if you choose to look at the big issues, recruit minds to look at the smaller issues for you." "If you choose to look at the smaller issues, recruit minds to look at the big issues for you."

12. The media reports of refugee calamity, but the architects see a work in progress. Always look at the big picture.

13. Of all the divine drugs for healing both the body and soul, laughter seems to be among the top class. It is said once a day is best. Bless those who make you laugh. Thank them profusely. Welcome them into your home regularly. O yes, say hello to jesters and comedians.

14. Only dialogue can pave the way to mutual understanding, harmony and secure a lasting peace. But the path to dialogue is sometimes fraught with bumps, chaos, and sometimes unwilling incidences.

15. Why do you fight with victors over the written course of history and legends therefrom? Do they not write history? Do losers write history? The next time you go into a war, make sure you win.

16. One planet, different worlds. One humanity, different laws and moral codes. What is unacceptable in one world is a code of honour in another. What is a crime in one world is acceptable in another. Where does the common law lie? Who is the judge of all? This is the cause of many wars. That by the colour of my skin I am different from my brother? That by manner of my tongue I am different? What if humanity is denoted by genetic definition; would there not be fewer wars? Or would humanity not stick together and fight our common enemies?

17. House of Destinies;
17.1. Before the LORD, souls pray,
17.2. Before Him, souls receive charges and lay out our Course,

17.3. Some pray for a desired course to come and make the world a better place,

17.4. Some crawl to the throne to pray profusely for a new destiny.

17.5. Some pray for the periodic calls for assignments of choice, they alone can honour.

17.6. The LORD asks, "Who would enter the world of mortals to bring my course?"

17.7. Souls rise to honour, but the LORD makes His own choice, and they descend to become our luminaries.

17.8. He sends them to the hell house of mortals, and humanity.

17.9. Some are born to special purpose,

17.10. Others are born to herald the message of light,

17.11. Others are born to suffer as testimonies,

17.12. All souls are in the house, praying, yearning and waiting for call,

17.13. All lifting their heads when the Time of "send" is upon the House.

17.14. "Send me O LORD....I am ready...I am ready...I would pay the price...I would not fail..." day and night, years unending they pray.

17.15. The LORD hears and turns his heard round, His Time in His hands to give a nod.

17.16. The LORD always hears.

17.17. It is an hour of jubilation when a soul is told, "you would descend into the world of mortals and ascend the glory of THE MOST HIGH",

17.18. All respond, "THE LORD IS ETERNAL, HIS WILL FOR MAN IS PERFECT AND GOOD."

17.19. The chosen Soul receives commendations and his fellow travellers pat him on the back, saying, "YOU SHALL DESCEND AND ASCEND TO BRING HEALING AND GLORY OF THE MOST HIGH."

17.20. The house sings well into Time, knowing that glory would be to the Messenger when he comes home. His reward enormous.

17.21. They share in his elevation giving glory to The LORD.

17.22. The LORD gives destinies as He charges,

17.23. He gives as it honours divine plan,

17.24. All pass through,

17.25. The House of Destinies holds the last nod, to all mortals.

18. What makes God good and the Devil evil when all demands sacrifices? What makes one evil or good when misfortune, pain, and tears characterise all followers? What is good about God when children gnash their teeth all their lives for bread? Those who have stood on both playgrounds, say, "GOD is good. All the time, He is."

19. What is grace when one has to pay a price? How is salvation a grace when one has to believe? Is belief not a higher price to pay than any amount of money could measure? Is reaching to a higher self an act of grace?

20. Why would the God of heaven, of love, of peace, of bliss, and of all which is good, take mortal man through a journey at the end of which, the man is left but with ruthlessness, anger and all sense of mercy, painfully burnt out of him? Ananse says, "that you would understand to be generous, be merciful and learn. Your choices are yours. Your will is yours."

21. Unconsciousness is a protector, a blinding veil and a cover for innocence. Many Champions have achieved great feats without knowing how great they have become. Long after the deeds are done and the vultures have fed on them and after the parrots have talked their tongues out from every detail of their deeds; long after the masses have been fed on these deeds, in the solemn and calmness of their rest, it would begin to dawn on these Champions what they have done. In that realisation, life would spring forth to fatten their bones knowing that they have once given hope to many. They have inspired so many and out of their deeds, a thousand champions were born. This is the true pride that those who boast should sing of. That, their deeds begot better and greater deeds. That, men of honour were born therefrom and generations were fed with hopes, wisdom, and honour from their deeds. Their codes were honour, dignity, hard work and sacrifice.

22. Getting to the top is never easy but Ananse has been told, "staying at the top is something else."

23. The night hunters;
23.1. Here they come.
23.2. Hear them coming.
23.3. The night has fallen and their cages have been opened.
23.4. Here they come, menacing, gasping and leaping from one end to the other through their dark underground alleys to sweep through the lands.
23.5. They come to devour the unprotected;
23.6. They come to devour their happiness, wealth and treasures.
23.7. And sow further seeds of strife, hunger, wickedness, poverty and all that keep man dreads of.
23.8. The LORD allows them to devour, for man has what weapons necessary to protect and be passed-over.
23.9. Hear them coming.
23.10. Nothing would halt them till they have gone through the lands.
23.11. Leaving on their trails dreaded waste.
23.12. At sunset clothe yourself with gratitude and reflections;
23.13. At night, flow in the potent powers of prayers and supplications.
23.14. Go to bed with shields of love, forgiveness, and truth.
23.15. Let these watch over you.
23.16. Let them protect you from those who ride in the night and devour all without walls and seals.
23.17. Call on GOD;
23.18. Call on His shield;
23.19. Call on Him six times a day and a final time before resting your bones.
23.20. Wakeup blessed and be truly blessed O protected One.

24. In the real world and on the battlefield, your potential does not matter. What matters and counts for much, is your skill. Fitness comes from training and practice.

25. You fool. You read books, consume the news and you think

you know this world. Come out of your cocoon and behold the world of man and you would regret God ever created that species. Continue to live under the wings of God and live. Come out and have your world shatter and behold the nightmare of all sages and teachers.

26. Sometimes you join the devils to make their evil plans less painful for man. Should you be judged for this? Would God declare "you are not my son?"

27. Ananse asks, "What were you told during the last battles for your entry into the world of man? What song were you charged to sing? Do you remember it? Has this flesh overcome your charge? Remember and bring healing to a troubled world.

28. The act happened before it happened. The act happened before you felt it. The act happened before you experienced it. Ananse puts it this way, "The material is the last face of all acts in the round of firsts."

29. Ananse speaks to the wayward woman, whose fleeting beauty of the flesh has become her weapon. "When I look at you, I see a weapon. It is very potent but would be short-lived. You may succeed by it but for a short while. Very soon this beauty you so rely on, would fade. A time would come when you would neither have the desire nor the energy to use it. Would you believe me if I say, I love you? I do. Hear my words and you would guide your soul. I have better weapons for you. They are more lasting, more potent and dignified. They are Knowledge and Wisdom. Embrace them and you would forever shine. They would stay with you long after your flesh has lost its vigour."

30. O LORD, the tent is ready for habitation. The song has been sung. The mind is ready; the tongue is sanctified; the man has now become the abode of GOD for His purpose for man. He is beautiful. He is yearning for your presence. He has read the vows. He has said the words. He is ready for greatness. He has sanctified himself from poison and filth.

# Chapter

*Ignorance of the invisible lines,*
*leads you to the doors of poverty, slavery and frustrations*

1. See yourself as more of a son or daughter of the nation than a child of an ethnic group. This is the bond which holds our nation together.

2. There are real but invisible Walls within every Society. Know them and you shall thrive. Ignore them and you would be a victim of ignorance.

3. There are latent and perpetual wars in every society. You can either join a faction or start your own war.

4. In a society of abundance of opportunities, there could be no limit to your rise. So help in creating opportunities. It is self-serving.

5. There is a perpetual struggle between new ideas and old beliefs. The new winning the war is never in doubt. The puzzle is how and when it would win.

6. Change does not come on a silver platter. Neither is it achieved from empty rhetoric or from the hallowed voices of conmen but by genuine struggles of blood and tears from noble and decent hearts.

7. To seek reform is to seek war. Know your turf and blast off.

8. Transformation of society has always been met with resistance. That is pretty obvious. What is critical is the fact that it takes a society to transform itself. There are no supermen or geniuses. There is only a humble leader and a little man.

9. Use of violence is unacceptable in any endeavour unless the other side fires the first bullet. In this, you only shoot back in self-defence.

10. Is resorting to violence justified in situations where all avenues of peaceful redress are deliberately blocked? Yes if your life and freedoms are threatened.

11. Blind ambition is suicidal. All ambitions should be guided by skill and common sense.

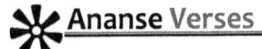 

12. Know the time to quit. Staying on longer than necessary defeats the purpose.

13. Both the old and the young view each other with suspicion.

14. In the battle of the ages, the young sees his agitation as a mark of liberation whereas the old sees his course of action as a mark of preservation.

15. Change always wins. It has never lost. So if you would choose a friend, embrace Change.

16. The fight for reforms is sometimes neither seen nor even heard loudly. It is sometimes a whisper, murmured at the lecture halls, in the commuter buses, at the marketplaces, or even in the bathrooms, in the ghettos, at the backhouses and some-times by those in the heat of the sun around the traffic lights selling pineapples, plantain chips, pens, dog chains and skip-ping ropes.

17. The greatest weapon is neither the sword nor the pen. The greatest weapon is the sword within. Find it and you would be a galactic warrior; use it for good and you would sit at the right hand side of The MOST HIGH.

18. It starts, goes round, returns and starts over again,

18.1. Is there any experience worse than paying for a bad food, eating a part of it, getting sick and bed ridden?

18.2. As you lie in pain, the health inspector goes to the bank for his salary

18.3. The politician who is taxing you to death rides in a motor-cade to cut a sod to the drilling of a borehole,

18.4. So your wife is late in delivering your food to you because the motorcade of the politician created a traffic jam,

18.5. The medical doctors are on strike for non-payment of extra duty allowance,

18.6. The nurses are on Skype,

18.7. The administrators are on Facebook,

18.8. The security guards chat on WhatsApp.

18.9. Meanwhile, the restaurant you ate from continues to do business!

19. Very soon, the world would be told religion is evil. It is devil worship. I wonder if we are not even at that point in history. It is not. It has merely become one, plaguing humanity and her followers. And there would be moments of anxiety and absolute sense of loss. The MAN who knows himself and his GOD would live and glorify the GOD of heaven and be happy.

20. So we watch them benignly as they create their world. That world of control and dominion. A world many call, "The police state." Terrorism they have created is their tool; terrorists they have trained, their weapons.

# Chapter

*Seek greater heights.*
*Seek loftier goals.*
*Claim higher grounds.*
*They are your rights as God's Child*

1. The wise and the most learned person is the lifelong student.

2. There is nothing so painful as to see your talents unexplored, dreams slipping through your fingers through lack of opportunities, hopelessness and stupor thriving while age, apathy, indifference and an uneven environment create the platform for only a few to excel.

3. Do not excel at the expense of others. There is no honour in it. The world would tell you it is smart. Ananse says, "There is neither honour nor dignity in it."

4. Not to have a dream, drive and abilities is one thing, but to have them and yet be prevented by your environment and circumstances is not only painful but also torturing.

5. At the point of desperation, do not turn bitter, do not fold up, just keep moving.

6. Is the end in sight? Hang on. There would be a way out, as there always is.

7. If you would go down, do so in dignity.

8. Create your own path to success if the society says NO to you.

9. If you would fight for something, fight for your beliefs.

10. Ananse says, "Politicians are not your friends. More and more, they are your competitors and exploiters."

11. The world is different now because of Technology. Make the most of it but beware of it downside.

12. The lure of wild dreams does not stand the test of time and reality. Neither does it appreciate tedious struggles of your mind and body nor the harsh realities of time and the environment. Be modest. Be wise and you would conquer.

13. Teamwork mostly pays off but good leaders are indispensable.

14. Without adequate skills you would loose out even if a billion opportunities are created, and dumped on you.

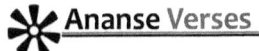

Only those with skills could benefit from available opportunities.

15. There is always a wide gap between awareness and reality.

16. Understanding a problem is the first part of solving it. Solving it is a logical sequence.

17. There is always a common ground in every disagreement. Seek it and you would find peace.

18. Times, seasons and man are partners-one a student, the other the master of all.
18.1. Times and seasons bind us all.
18.2. Your time of peace is my time of war;
18.3. Your time of war is my time of peace.
18.4. Your time of peace is his time of war;
18.5. So could his time of peace be your time of war.
18.6. Our time of peace could be his time of war,
18.7. As his time of war, my time of peace.
18.8. So we are bound to behave differently to situations.
18.9. Understanding this and behaving accordingly to each other is the proper way to live and prosper under the common banner of Time.
18.10. A single thread called time binds us all.

19. The society knows whom it has given so much to. She knows whom she has given little to and whom she has given nothing to. Mostly, those she has given much to are not her well-behaved children.

20. The curse of Ananse;
20.1. He saw wisdom and the glory therefrom and he chose.
20.2. He saw the fluidity of the self yet he chose wisdom,
20.3. One time an angel, at another a pervert, yet he chose wisdom to embrace this fluid;
20.4. At one moment a man of honour and teacher of humanity and at another, a childish brute sobbing from the flesh, yet he chose wisdom.
20.5. Would be hated yet he chose;

20.6.  Hated, yet he held on to her.

20.7.  He is not blind to who he has become or the price he paid.

20.8.  He simply chose to be wise knowing that, you cannot exist in the flesh and hold that wisdom without being what he has become.

20.9.  Perpetually, a single step from fall.

21.   A prayer for emancipation;

21.1.  We cry to our God,

21.2.  We wail and groan to our saviour,

21.3.  Our shame burdens us,

21.4.  Our humiliation knows no bound.

21.5.  We cry onto you O Father,

21.6.  We cry onto you O Mother,

21.7.  We commit ourselves to walk the journey,

21.8.  We commit our children to walk the journey,

21.9.  And hold the sword of war.

21.10.  We commit our lands to the cause,

21.11.  We commit our rivers to parity,

21.12.  We commit our souls O Lord.

21.13.  Walk through our lands and heal us,

21.14.  Lead us and be our LORD,

21.15.  Deliver and restore us,

21.16.  And lead us to the dream.

22.   I paid for the wealth;

22.1.  I saw wealth and beheld it.

22.2.  He opened the chest and saw a consuming fire,

22.3.  I saw worlds therefrom;

22.4.  I did not hesitate;

22.5.  I plunged my fist in and I was absorbed and consumed.

22.6.  I came out not as flesh and blood,

22.7.  I came out a spirit, of wealth.

22.8.  But I had no need of the wealth because I lived in a new world,

22.9.  A world where the material wealth of this earth has no place.

23.  A world not our own;

23.1.  What world have we created?

23.2.  What world have we been sold to?

23.3.  What world has been thrust upon us?

23.4.  That we have no light in sight nor hope therein?

23.5.  Who created it?

23.6.  Who created man and left us to scream therein?

23.7.  A world of needs; a world of wants; a world of loss.

# Chapter

*Sometimes all it takes to heal body and soul, is a good music*

1. Know your limitations and act accordingly; acknowledge the potentials of others, and learn from them and you would be a better person.

2. Most people believe in what they are fighting for, even if they are wrong.

3. God lives in you. He is in your genes. You only have to allow Him to be your master. Surrender and obey his voice.

4. No matter your weaknesses, deficiencies and fears, remember that you are central to the development of your community. Whatever skill or resources you have is necessary for your society's development. See how useful jesters are to even kings!

5. Grow with time; change with your environment and you would forever be useful to your society. Be static and you would surely die a gradual and painful death.

6. Change starts in the mind, so is transformation but maturity comes with experiences and time.

7. O man, know where you come from and prepare yourself for home. Cut out the poison. Stop the consumption of poison and conserve your energies for the next journey.

8. Your culture can inhibit your development or promote the same. It is all about a slight change of perspective.

9. You would always lack something. What matters is the ability to appreciate your deficiency and be a continual learner.

10. Life begins at forty (40) to someone, to another it begins at twenty-five (25) and still to others, seventeen (17). Know your time and flow with it.

11. Know yourself and you shall prosper.

12. You can cheat in your examinations and secure a certificate but you can never cheat life. You would surely be exposed.

13. You learn most by participating.

14. Be a friend to hope till you are matured to understand the curses of reality.

15. Successful people dream and go to work. Losers dream and sleep.

16. Education is about understanding, reading, communication, common sense and a change in character for the better.

17. You are never a product of accidents so do not leave your life to chance.

18. If you would fail, fail by attempting to avoid failure. In that case, even if you fail, you can take pride in being the architect of your own failure.

19. If you would succeed, succeed by not failing to succeed.

20. If you would fail, fail by not failing to avoid failure. If you would succeed, succeed by succeeding to succeed.

21. When you fail by not failing to avoid failure, there would be no one to save you but only Fortune himself. And fortune does not suffer fools. As you succeed, know that, you might have failed over and over again. That is how life sometimes rewards poor mortals.

22. Do not deceive yourself with your toys. You are a mortal and God is God. Having a glimpse at His realm does not make you God or God less than He is.

23. Character is the constitution of habits and attitudes.

24. I have a job, let me do my job. You have a job, do your job. If we allow each other to honour our jobs, we shall move forward. And with that forward move would come happiness and fulfilment.

25. Do not leave the task of your development to someone. Take control of your destiny.

26. We are the product of our environment and time.
    But we cannot disregard character.

27. As you criticise one generation today, note that one day, another generation would rise to criticise you. So be modest and honest.

28. You should not be guided only by the successes of earlier generations but their failures as well. Their failures would make you wiser.

29. Believe in your society but do not be her donkey. If anyone would be her donkey, let it be those who control her resources.

30. Time may influence dreams so beware and change accordingly. Watch time closely and you would understand her turns and twists. She brings in its wake new opportunities, benefits and challenges.

31. Every generation has its challenges, trials, temptations and call.

32. The tools of survival of one generation might be obsolete in relation to new and emerging challenges facing another generation.

33. How just, prompt and merciless time is;
33.1. A time comes when everyone has to quit.
33.2. A wise man would know when to quit.
33.3. Therein lies the mark of his wisdom.
33.4. The limitations of human strength, weakness and desire, make it more important for older generations to, at a point in time, give way to a new and energetic generation to carry on. Ananse says, "This too is a command from time."
33.5. No single generation can fight forever nor deliver the promise.
33.6. So the wise generation would know what her obligations are and fetter accordingly.

34. Tell yourself the truth. Face the truth and grow into Freedom.

35. True love does not know death, neither does she taste pain, anger or hunger; all that she knows is Love. And when all else is done and gone, she would still remain. Love is not crowded

by circumstances. She is not consumed by Time. She remains forever from once cycle to the other. Forever remaining to feed her children.

36. Love is sexless. Truth is a hermaphrodite, Mercy is a female and Justice is a he.

37. Failures do not try. Or as Ananse would put it, "failures give up easily."

38. The beautiful ones are out of sight. They always are. You have to search for them, look for them and when you find them, they are always worth the search.

39. O Children, Ananse weeps for you. Why do you limit your horizon to what you see, hear, touch or smells? Free your mind to the divine and you would behold a glorious world beyond this prison called flesh and blood.

40. The wise cries all day. Who cries more than the wise? He hears folly; he sees madness; he smells waste and feels nothing worth the standard of he who is called MAN. So cries at man wasting himself off. Children pursuing vanity all their lives. They eat and drink poison and call it food.

41. Wisdom is the ultimate weapon of the wise. It is his key to the court of kings and a seat among savers of the city. It is a lifelong asset. So Ananse cries, "O children, lose everything but gain wisdom. Sacrifice your all for her and in her bosom, you would find wealth, grace, honour, and power; with these, what else is impossible for you to have?"

42. The journey of life has huge bottlenecks. The journey of life has landmarks; the journey has strange stories, which add up to define the life that is, was and would be.

43. "What should the Masters do when you have two equally strong forces fighting to the death and destroying everything in the process?" Ananse was asked. He responded, "You have seven options";

43.1. Seek resolution by dialogue,

43.2. Allow the course of their folly to come to full cycle

43.3. Reduce their capabilities so that after their madness, there would be something left to build on.

43.4. Judge them. Declare support for the one with the just cause and support him to triumph.

43.5. Support the one with the highest potential even if he has a less appealing case. In that case, let the other retire to an old age with pride.

43.6. Support none but destroy them both.

43.7. Remove the cause of the conflict and kill the instinct in them which is driving their madness.

43.8. Herein the actors must choose wisely.

# Chapter

*I owe no debt to the god of religion*
*The MOST HIGH GOD holds my debts*
*He sets out the freedom and salvation of all without colour or airs.*
*That by religion, my brother who is the blood of my father and the fluid*
*of my mother*
*Has become my enemy,*
*A hatred creature because he is a Muslim, Christian or Hindu?*

1. Do not sell lies;
    1.1. A lie has a life of its own.
    1.2. A lie grows.
    1.3. A time would surely come when it becomes so appealing that it is believable.
    1.4. At that point, it has already become a poisoned and sharpened arrow ready to destroy you first, and then all who believe it,
    1.5. And if unlucky, the whole society as we know it.

2. When a season comes and desire gives way and you are no longer challenged to do anything, know that it is time to bow out and take full credit for your work. If you stay, you risk losing it all.

3. Leaders of men are no saints. And so could saints not be leaders of men.

4. Some leaders could be a threat to your development. Neither becomes their puppet nor their enemy.

5. Creating the balance in your life calls for wisdom. Your ability to create a balance tells you, you are wise and matured. Your inability to create the balance should tell you, you are still a child needing great wealth of learning and guidance.

6. Remember your fathers at all times. Remember your mother always. Remember their words; remember their fears; remember their love, rebukes, scolding and cares. It is all you need in your journey of life.

7. In your time of comfort remember those in peril. In your time of peril remember your values.

8. There is a natural glitch in any act of goodness. God would not hold you accountable. Ananse says, "There is a consequence to every good action." It is either on you or someone else. So beware! When you set out to farm, you are likely to destroy the home of the ants; when you set out to build your house, you are likely to destroy someone's farm.

9. The young must learn; sometimes they do so by listening; sometimes they do through painful experiences.

10. Traditions are a foundation. They are more of a guide than a rule. They should be seen in the light of the day not as they meant yesterday.

11. Abuse the young ladies and you would be abusing the next generation of our leaders.

12. Prayer works. It is the ultimate weapon that God has given man. It protects, heals, pulls down, and builds.

13. In a society of scarce opportunities, it is most difficult to preach virtues. How can a hungry man think straight; how do people who have no bread comprehend the lore of virtue?

14. When life is on the balance, survival is likely to come first before values.

15. Dance hall kings in the palaces of leadership;
15.1. "Our youth have been caged and placed on the slave market whilst our leaders dance "Azonto".
15.2. Our young ladies are stripped naked before us and we marvel lustfully at their bulging shiny breasts and bodies, forgetting that at their demise, our society comes to an end.
15.3. Ananse says, "For the sake of our humanity, let us educate our youth."
15.4. "Let us teach them who they are."
15.5. "Teach them what a great race they come from."
15.6. "Teach them where they are going."
15.7. "Let us tell them the codes of wisdom and with them, they would establish their happy destinies."

16. From where we stand today;
16.1. Our professionals are corrupted.
16.2. They see good as evil and corruption as the way of God.
16.3. So we cannot go forward.
16.4. How do we move forward?
16.5. I say, "Let us train a new breed of professionals."

16.6.  Ananse says, "Select and execute the existing professionals."

16.7.  "Execute them first, then you can train new breeds."

16.8.  I say, "Too brutish"

16.9.  Ananse responds, "You are too naïve."

16.10. "If you leave the old stocks of depraved professionals alive, they would corrupt the new breed and all our efforts would come to naught."

16.11. And I say, "If you remove these pigs at a time when there is no replacement, we would design our own fall."

16.12. Ananse responds, "Train a new breed of leaders in batches, execute the old rotten oranges in batches."

17.  You fool, do not close your eyes to the plight of the poor; your mind sees, and your conscience cries. You cannot escape your responsibilities.

18.  Dignity, such a powerful protector. Do not sell her for anything. Do not lose her if you wish to be respected in the council of your peers.

19.  Beauty is a weapon for good and evil;

19.1.  Able to disarm the warrior and bring healing to the madman.

19.2.  Whoever uses her beauty for good would be loved and respected.

19.3.  Whoever uses her beauty for evil would have her flesh eaten,

19.4.  And her inner-self despised and destroyed.

19.5.  In the end, she would lose it all.

20.  Groan in your pain, for it reminds your soul that you are in the healing chamber but do not moan in your pleasure. It irritates the soul.

21.  Nation wreckers gathered to celebrate their greatest kills, but their appetites were so insatiable that they turned on one another.

22.  Let us start learning all over again as a nation. The old is dead. It did not save us. It brought us pain and destruction. Ananse prays, "Let us be born again."

23. In a sick society, your talent could be your curse. Beware of whom you allow to come close to you. Beware of whom you share your dreams with.

24. Talent, skill, boldness and commitment should back your drive and motivation. Without these, the talent would only become a mirror disconnected from your dreams.

25. Knowing and growing;
    25.1. Young brilliant men have lost so much because at the wrong time, they talked.
    25.2. Know when to speak.
    25.3. Know where to speak.
    25.4. Know how to speak.
    25.5. It is all about learning and growing into maturity.

26. A big shame, when I hear the living says, "It is over." It is never over even when you lie lifeless; someone would pick up your dreams.

27. Do not forget the values, which brought you success in the first place. Hold on to them even tighter when you believe to have succeeded. Transform them but never dilute them nor compromise them.

28. A piece of paper or a ring of gold does not guarantee freedom. Freedom comes from within. Claim it and live and you would not be hindered in any dimension.

29. Fear the future if your leaders are gluttons. Fear the future if you cannot stop them. Fear the future if you are blind and leprous.

30. Politics may have failed you but you are not a failure. Not yet. You are the only one who can guarantee your failure and I know you would choose success because the price you would pay for failure is greater than what success is asking for.

31. The society you live in is your creation. So if it is a great society then be proud. Otherwise, bow your head in shame.

32. Mankind would always migrate to where opportunities are. So do not erect iron walls, or construct landmine parameters. Create opportunities; build a society fit for living and the people would come. Nor would they attempt to escape."

33. When Failure knocks on your door for a visit, shake his hands, look at him in the eyes and tell him you have only one seat and Success has already taken it.

34. Of the Ananse Verses, the wise look at it and increase in wisdom; the young look at it and drink more than necessary but would survive; the old look at them and rest, but the fool would only look at it and ask, "Who is Ananse?"

35. Listen to him; he says he is the President. He believes he presented a manifesto, went to the people, the people voted for his wisdom, the votes were counted and he was declared the President Elect, so he says, "I am the President..." He does not know who the real presidents are.

36. Oh, have you not noticed the changes around? Those days when you go to school, come out and look up to the government for jobs, are over. They are not coming back. The new employers of the age are yourself and the mean animal called the private sector. Stop fighting the government for jobs.

37. Where are the men with common sense? As knowledge is said to have increased exponentially, I only hear narrow minds. Lawyers want to make every issue a legal one; Economists make every issue an economic issue; Medical Doctors make every issue a medical one and Accountants reduce every issue to accounting ratios. Narrow minds...so embarrassing and helpless outside their areas of so-called specialty.

38. Wisdom is everywhere. Open your eyes, observe, learn and apply.

39. Be relentless in learning and gaining wisdom; for when adversity comes, you would be the only one on the dance floor. That is

where your wisdom would count. Woe onto you if you do not have enough.

40. There are different classes of people by virtue of your orientation, dreams, environment and place in the society. So are our thinking and opinions. Be who you are. Never be what the society wants you to be. It might not be who you are born to be.

41. A message to crusaders and believers;
41.1. Do you wish to change the world?
41.2. Change yourself first;
41.3. Change your ways;
41.4. Change your attitudes,
41.5. Then from the new self, you would have the strength to go forward.
41.6. These are Ananse's words to every Crusader.

42. Some people have opportunities thrust upon them by blood and association. Others stumble upon them; others create their own through blood and sweat. In all, look to God and never turn from a righteous life and the plight of the poor.

43. The graces of God bring blessings and there is no bitter taste afterwards.

44. Of Slaves and Freemen. There are some people who work all day to only make it to their mouths. Others work only four hours a day and drive home in a Bugatti with surpluses to spare for a year.

45. There are those who even in their poverty could buy nations because they dreamt, set their horizons high and worked hard with a clear conscience. They know that wealth has nothing to do with paper currency. It is something within; it is fluid, subtle and spiritual. Know this and you would thrive.

46. Your choices could throw your life away. Be wise!

47. Without wisdom and hard work, luck would elude you.

48. Eagles, through sheer work, toil, commitment and God's grace and favour, have realised their dreams. Who are you? A parrot or an opportunist?

49. Share a belief in divine favour but remember to earn your daily bread as a man.

50. Work hard, sacrifice and bid your time and you would rise to the top.

51. Do not take more than you need. It would become a burden to you.

52. Do not be someone else's pet receiving cramps from his table. You would blunt your greatness. Be your own man. Be the eagle you can be and from the mountaintop, soar even higher and feed multitudes.

# Chapter

*From today, I cease to be responsible for others' wealth*
*And irresponsible to myself.*
*From today, I turn the lights to my well being;*
*I create greatness for myself;*
*I make myself the lord of wealth.*
*I decree them and humbly,*
*I shall be presented to the Throne of Destinies,*
*at the feet of the Ancient of Days*
*For canonisation*

1. An easy life kills your initiative. It robs you of greatness and attempts to cheat life. Life would definitely have his say.

2. Life is never a straight path. Even though it rises and falls deep into a valley, it is crooked in every sense of the word. Till you hit the cycle and are carried in the frequencies, you are a tortured, haunted and confused creature. Ananse can only pity you. It is the only way out for all who seek to conquer.

3. Some actions must be done in the way they have to be done. There is no other way.

4. From afar, I see the mountain Afadjato rise up so majestically. When I stood at her base, I could see valleys in her majestic rise. Keep moving. You may be in a valley; yes, in a valley but it is the way upward.

5. For some fellows, life is meaningful to them in the sense that, they have had streams of opportunities without a setback? When reality says hello to them, then they begin to cut corners and groan, causing all sorts of harm to God's planet. You are a weakling. Be strong. You have the strength to be strong.

6. Hold your self in the midst of setbacks; keep your calm; lift your head up and say to yourself, "I am in a flow."

7. Stop whining! Wake up, stand up and be a man.

8. A life well lived is rewarding but it is never smooth. So stop chewing your tongue. Those at the top were here not long ago.

9. Do not live on charity. There is neither dignity nor pride in it.

10. All life is scripted. All songs are noted down. Would you sing your song?

11. Entrepreneurship is hell, and then fulfilment and the rewards follow.

12. Beware of what you dream of. In your comfortable cocoon you claim to rule the world. What would you do when this shell burst and you see that you are one of seven billion poor mortals?

13. According to Ananse, "Inspiration is a strange being." In a moment he gives you the abilities to conceive the impossible.

14. Do not cut corners. It would come back to bite you at a time you have no strength to defend yourself. It would come back to bite you the moment you say, "It is time to rest."

15. Do not offset the balance of society. Your very survival depends on the balance.

16. Get close to the centre of power. There are lots of rewards therein. But when you do, be cunning, be of good virtue or else your life would be short and painful.

17. Never accept anything on a silver platter. It may be a trap or the price for it would be your dignity.

18. How beautiful it is to live your old age in peace and comfort. Would there be something more rewarding?

19. If you live in a society where your life is more in danger for doing good, then know that, your society is heading towards a crash; abandon it or fight for a re-birth, else all would come down crumbling with a deafening sound. O, do not be surprised if the masses, forever fooled, continue their life in ignorance as the crash begins and gathers steam.

20. If something does not belong to you, neither take it nor accept it. By taking it for yourself, you may bring sadness to someone.

21. Accept the best if you are the best. Refuse it if offered for free. Always work for what you want.

22. Beware. Proximity to abundance and comfort makes one soft. Always remember that, you live in a cruel and unfriendly world.

23. "Leadership comes with authority and those to be entrusted with power must themselves be in a position to appreciate the implications and consequences of their decisions."

24. There are many things in this life that obviously neither books nor story telling can bestow on you. You may read all the books

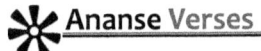

and biographies of great men about life, but for one to appreciate them in a realistic manner, is for one to live them.

25. Live and die for a good cause.

26. Today's failures could be tomorrow's successful persons.

27. Twelve to one; twenty-four to three or five; thirty-six to many. There are always traitors around, so watch your back.

28. Not all of us could withstand hunger or thirst.

29. Whereas some people sweat through life, others float through it.

30. Sometimes loyalty is the price of comfort. At other times the price is death.

31. Some people may seem to care but if you look at them critically, it is all about pretences.

32. Sell yourself cheap through life today, and tomorrow you cannot pay the asking price for your freedom tomorrow.

33. Are you a pet being fed from a silver spoon? Are you looking for easy food and perks? O, what a cheap person. Look at how you have become an object of amusement! Ananse urges, "Refuse to be one." If you are already one, change. Earn your daily bread and with it would come respect.

34. Sometimes, to see the light, it is simply about change of orientation and perspective.

35. Find a route for your dreams. Do not resign to the base of the ladder. Remember never to trust chance. Chance is only favourable to those who prepare and work their way up.

36. Sometimes, failure is unavoidable. What matters is what you do when you are down.

37. Servants look for a master to serve. A leader guides the masses to the Promised Land.

38. You can change your situation if you have the right levels of anger, pain and purpose.

39. Turn your experience into wealth and stop whining.

40. Survivors never see a dead end. They are always knocking and peeping.

41. Some are successful by accident of birth, others by good hand of fortune. But if you were born into a valley, you would have to create your own success.

42. Misfortune moves at the speed of light but fortune rides on the back of a tortoise.

43. If you would have a friend, have Time as your best friend even if he is a pain sometimes because she always brings healing and settlement.

44. Society is not the enemy. It is the image of the enemy.

45. Dragging your feet on a matter would only make your case worse. Quicken your steps and meet whatever is on the horizon.

46. There comes a time when a straw is more valuable than the cord of the climber.

47. Do not live your dream at the expense of others. They would come at you in arms and you may not survive.

48. We are not cowards; we do not run from battle cries; we do not freeze at the sight of our enemies. We are simply waiting for the right war; the right enemy, then we shall fight.

49. Sometimes all that is needed to end a gathering battle is to show the sword. No need to draw; no need to spill blood.

# Chapter

*If I picked paupers and made them millionaires,*
*I can make myself a billionaire.*
*I make myself a billionaire at this hour now and here.*
*My hands are blessed; my intentions for riches are noble.*
*I hope to stand noble till the end of my days.*

1. Hate luck and despise him with all your might. The only guys you should love are hard work and Divine favour.

2. When it goes well for you, laugh your heart out but laugh the more when it goes against you. After all what can you do? Misfortune has already happened.

3. Show me a man who has never made a mistake in life and I would show you the source of the sea.

4. Build upon your strengths even if you consider they are insignificant in the larger scheme of things. They could be your only routes to the table of Kings. I saw the note-taker comfortably seated at the right hand side of the king whilst the Finance Minister strains his neck to be seen.

5. Some people rise to the top by attaching themselves to the establishment. Others by reward of loyalty and still others by their own hands.

6. I see the messenger go to the king's private chamber without an appointment whilst Governors wait for months for audience.

7. Learn to do things by yourself. There is pride in it. Learn to dress your bed; learn to wash your clothes; learn to iron your clothes. There is pride in them.

8. We need the little man so that the big man would be unmistaken.

9. Seek peace most in the time of peace.

10. How much can you do? Concentrate your energies on what you have to do.

11. We need men with the tongue of wisdom to bring some level of calmness and peace to a troubled youth.

12. In times of stress and fear and confusion, all that matters most is calmness and a soft voice.

13. Eagles are rare. They are the pioneers upon whose shoulders

the burden of leadership, responsibility and pain of failure and or success lie.

14. Do not forget the words of the sages. They are institutions of divine order. What immovable shoulders they are.

15. There is a proper procedure for doing everything. If not followed, peace, victory or fulfilment cannot be guaranteed.

16. The strength of the warrior is in his heart. Noise, wind or flames never move him. His strategies are ever evolving.

17. Leaders should be the protectors and servants of their generations.

18. Live above yourself and put the interests of your generation first. This is the safest route to earn dignity and respect among your people.

19. Sometimes we say, "leaders are irresponsible to themselves because they put the welfare of others above theirs." Well, maybe in that irresponsibility lies their fulfilment and rest. Should the people who benefit from their selflessness complain? Well, I can hear their families complaining in silence.

20. Dare to achieve the impossible.

21. Are you not tired of old ideas? It is time to break new grounds.

22. Do not believe in secondary knowledge and achievements. Identify what you want, plan for it, and pay the price required.

23. Let it not be your dream to take from the society more than you give back to her. That is your service to the land that nourished you with her milk. Give her more.

24. Give to the poor, help the weak and avoid the cheap ways.

25. We are all tested.

26. With the good that we do, evil men pick it up as a weapon against us and God on his throne watches till we are complete.

27. Ananse said, "The most silly job I have ever done is the President of this family." The greatest job I have ever done was being a teacher. Then he concluded, "If you seek a job for pleasure or ambition, that is vanity; but if you seek it for service to society and mankind, that is honourable."

28. Do not build your hope on the masses. Their marriage does not normally last long. They easily forget, and loyalty is not familiar to them.

29. Keep your head down. Keep your feet firmly rooted on the ground. Watch your steps keenly when all seems to be going well for you. This is the moment you are most prone to a fall.

30. On your way up, make more friends than enemies, for you do not know the hand which would welcome you when your days of glory are over.

31. Remember, the adoring crowd of today may hate and despise you tomorrow as much as they love and adore you today.

32. Do not solely rely on the strength and toils of others to survive. Make your own world and on your strength make your name.

33. Irrespective of what the society has given you, give much back to the society. If you take one from the society, give seven-fold back.

34. Know your limits. Do not act beyond it. It would only bring you pain and disappointments.

35. Do not fret when you become the target of small minds. It is in their nature to be little. Pursue your dreams.

36. Never be afraid to go against the status quo whatever the cost, as long as it serves a greater goal.

37. Your level of opposition carries a message. The greater your goals, the greater the opposition you face. No one cares about you if you are no threat to him or her.

38. There are many kinds of education. There is the education of Certificate and the education of Life. The education of certificate is a deception. The education of life is the toughest but all who dare go through become better persons.

39. It has to be done however painful. We destroy the cancer or it destroys us all. Our judge is GOD. He is merciful.

40. The pursuit of dreams requires sacrifice. Those who aspire for higher service and share of God's benevolence ought to commit much of themselves to their dreams with higher standards.

41. The dreams of great men will be the hope for a better tomorrow. Whilst in their challenges and trials, many find lifelong lessons and comfort. To little men, their dream is to seek their own little good at the expense of the society.

42. There are systems in every society and these systems have their protectors. You cannot rise to alter the systems without defeating the protectors. And you, Mr Dreamer, how would you know the Protectors?

43. Dreams alone are not enough to achieve your goals. You need wisdom, strength and foresight.

44. Most societies by nature of the human animal, do not like non-conformist. So the society would most likely oppose anyone who challenges the status quo.

45. There is conclusion to every matter. Your worry should be the sort of conclusion life would thrust upon you.

46. Sometimes a victory is neither the triumph of money nor fame but the triumph of conviction, purpose, drive, and belief.

47. Without war there would be no victory. Pain, suffering and bruises are all part of it.

48. Every society needs heroes. All societies do. Every society has her heroes.

49. You must know where you are going.

50. The meanness of little minds is irritating but the wise would ignore them.

51. The masses would normally oppose what is good for them.

52. The pursuit of Dreams and vision is always a lonely journey.

53. The will of progressive minds keep the society alive.

54. Wishes never build a kite.

55. It is only by living a life that you would come to appreciate it and sacrifice for greater goals. For within this sacrifice lies the essence of that life.

56. Glow and shine. You may be the light the society has been waiting for. This is your time.

57. Make a virtuous living from your beauty or survive on your voice, these are the gifts the Lord has blessed you with.

58. Sometimes life is about taking opportunities. Sometimes it is about the right judgement; sometimes it is about good counsel. It is never about folly or madness.

59. There are those who glow so fast and burn so quickly, and there are those who gloom through the billows of life and stay long.

60. Of all the weapons available to you, the cheapest is Silence; yet it is one of the most potent.

61. Ambition has trapped many a man in a cage of self-destruction. It has become a net of slavery and men of power, the cunning and wealthy, have used it to buy the souls of those trapped.

62. What do you do when you have nothing to say? Shut Up.

63. Experience is the greatest rod of life. It can change a docile pet into an agile and graceful eagle.

64. A new perspective can transform you beyond your imagination.

65. Young lad, note that "nothing," they say, "is permanent." As much as our society is dynamic in so many ways, so is each state. An experience can change a weakling into a sombre person. Therefore, a broken man can acquire new orientation and take a new course in life.

66. Define yourself, set your goals in life and be confident of what you want.

67. In today's environment of near hopelessness and rare opportunities to the African youth, the society and the government are the enemies of progress and prosperity.

68. To know yourself is to face life squarely; to be ignorant is to be blown back and forth by the storms this society has set in perpetual motion.

69. It is suicidal to set your foot into the real world if you do not know who you are or what you want.

70. Never leave anything to chance lest the environment would turn you into a product the society has no need of.

71. Life is about patience and timing. If you are too slow you would be left behind. If you rush, you would make fatal errors and be cast aside.

72. Life does not follow a straight path and knowledge acquired only through books does not guarantee success in life.

73. There is, as always, a wide and infinite gap between knowledge and reality. This gap is really important to you going forward. This is critical to you in building your patience, perseverance, and learning skills, attitudes and resources necessary in making a progressive and matured growth.

74. "My son is the next Einstein" Yes he may be. But Ananse says, "Wait till the Environment, Time, Society and the tolls of Life have spoken."

75. Of friends, allies, interests and security.

75.1. America is our major friend and our protector, but she is not enough for us,

75.2. We need other friends, not for protection from our enemies, alone, but from our major friend.

75.3. Beijing is the best other bet; for funding and protection and as a deterrent,

75.4. Of course Washington's interest may change as it often had;

75.5. Our other friends would provide us what our major friends cannot or are unwilling to provide,

75.6. Even in this, our benefactor friend, must know what we do lest our friendship suffers and we are braced;

75.7. Our intentions made clear,

75.8. Our moves not public but not too private to raise suspicion and create doubt;

75.9. Our friend must know, we need her, we respect her and are a willing learner and team player,

75.10. But we are no slaves, puppets nor drags.

75.11. We are simply trying to make a living and earn a place for our people;

75.12. Our resources and wealth we shall share evenly as each friend require and we can afford;

75.13. We shall not forget our enemies.

75.14. All hours, we shall keep an eye on them.

75.15. All hours, we shall engage, taking what we can learn.

75.16. And learning the best way to live with them.

75.17. Can our today's friends blame us for learning to understand our enemies?

75.18. What if they are so to us because we made a choice?

75.19. What if they become our friends tomorrow?

75.20. And our friends of today shall take their place tomorrow?

75.21. We shall be wise, there is no room for folly.

75.22. We shall be natural students, there is no room for arrogance;

75.23. We shall be fast learners because our curve is steep.

## Chapter

*If you can help people who depend on you to climb the Kilimanjaro,*
*Then you can climb the Everest by the hand of fortune*

1. Maturity is not a matter of age; it is a matter of understanding the ways of life and making decisions reminiscent of a wholesome human being.

2. Your decisions at every turn of your life should contribute to the attainment of your dreams and goals.

3. "Oh children, how long would you continue to be slaves to sensual and emotional surges? I hear you are killing one another over the flesh of a woman, and material wealth. Children, grow up and dine with me." These are the words Ananse heard from the throne of THE MOST HIGH.

4. I hear you are blinded by your senses? Wisdom asks.

5. The cunning one does not reveal himself. He is a different being to different people.

6. Knowing is one thing and actually having the acquired ability to execute what you know is another.

7. Do you know? Do you know that the distance between your dreams and their fulfilment could be forever?

8. Love your Nation. Above all Love your nation. Love the land that gave you a name and the breast of her women nourished you. Love the land you call your home. Love the land that protects you.

9. Sometimes, you may shout corruption, sycophancy, greed and bad policies. Until you are faced with the reality of these flaws, it would be difficult to appreciate the enormity of how enticing these weaknesses are.

10. Your point of reality is when you come face to face with it. Reality is not a dream. It is your life and the lives of many who look up to you.

11. Ooh reality how wicked you are; tearing people apart with your cold steel and breaking down their defences mercilessly.

12. Loyalty has her rewards in dignity.

13. Ananse says, "You are encouraged to listen, learn and sometimes pause to reconsider a lot of issues before making a decision or boisterously shouting at the top of your voice."

14. Every step you take in the real world could lead to a worse situation, your end, or lead you to a better situation.

15. It is important for you to acknowledge that it is one thing being aware of a situation, another thing understanding it, another having the skills and abilities to examine it and yet another having the courage, resources and the will to make a decision to attempt to solve it.

16. You think your fathers are failures? Wait till you are there. Be humble. Learn why they failed and you would successful.

17. It is a lot easy identifying the numerous 'evils' within our environment but a lot more complex and difficult in setting the environment right. This too is a reality. Ananse has no solution, except to say that, "Follow the wise, eat their words and you would laugh last and laugh long."

18. "Fighting and overcoming corruption and other vices which have torn our society apart is never easy. It takes time. It is a winding course. It is never an instantaneous act. It is not a sprint race. It is more of heptathlon of a marathon."

19. You need an army to conquer the demons of our society.

20. Every campaign calls for patience to pick up steam.

21. There is always so much to learn and much to prove if you are to be respected and if you are to sustain that respect.

22. Beware! Look and learn. Pause before you talk.

23. Grow up. We are in the 21$^{st}$ Century. Look at Africa for what we are today and not what you wish us to be or you have been educated to think about us. Stop reading those books about

us. If you would err, err by considering Africa for our coming greatness and we shall be generous. We are the Colossus.

24. In my mind, I lost but the world says I won; I am a realist. I believe it. In my heart I am like any other leader but the world says I am the greatest; I am humbled.

25. You succeeded because someone failed. Be humble. You succeeded because someone was forced to fail. Be wise. You succeeded because someone was set up to fail. Do not be a fool by being ignorant of the affairs of men.

26. Life has happy and sour moments, so remember the happy days when sour days sit face to face with you for a chat.

27. Life has its lows and joys for everyone. It is fraught with hurdles and roadblocks. Know this and you would embrace long life; ignore this and you would entangle yourself with webs of frustration and pain.

28. Life has a unique way of upsetting you. Do not fight it when it upsets you. Just flow with the storm.

29. Once my father told me, "My son read.... read... read everything that you find, even when you find texts from the refuse damp, for knowledge is the only thing which can save you." I took it to heart and today I love him for it because reading has brought me fortune and grace.

30. There is something you should take note of and prepare for. You may read the examination questions carefully, yet you may deviate from a question and provide the wrong answer. It is an occurrence of life. This life or any life you may know is full of stones.

31. One way or the other, we are all slaves to something: to our evil deeds, inclinations, dreams, and ambitions or even to our good intentions.

32. People who stumble and fall are neither toddlers nor cripples. They just missed a step and stumbled. Your

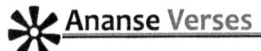 

test of strength and conviction lies in your rising again. When you rise, you become wiser, more careful and stronger.

33. My son, I was told:
33.1.   As you pursue your dreams in life, note that there are crises periods, which are devastating, crushing and cold.
33.2.   They are periods of uncertainty, confusion and complete darkness.
33.3.   They are periods when you question your own identity.
33.4.   They are periods when you no longer believe in yourself.
33.5.   They are periods of weakness and doubt when everything seems to be against you.
33.6.   They are periods of loneliness.
33.7.   Ananse says, "When you meet these moments, just smile in your pains and take it in your stride. They would pass."

34. Poverty drives away all friends but success and riches would bring them back. Ananse says, "Success always brings monsters and vultures around you."

35. Stand firm. It is only a storm. A storm you would one day look back at and smile at.

36. Do not be alarmed if you are alone. Your vision could be the beginning of a great thing for the nation.

37. The human body hates troubles and misfortunes but they are good for the soul. They are tests of manhood. When it is all over, you surely have to be a better person: disciplined, humble and hardworking. For fools, Ananse says that, "They would complain and cry over and over, till they are consumed by their complaints."

38. Believe in your dreams.

39. Do not give up. Do not lose hope. Focus. Pray and tap into the abundance of God.

40. Most people who set out to achieve their lofty dreams have found themselves one point or the other at a stage of con-

fusion. Those moments are periods of tests. Keep your eyes on the dream and move up; lose focus and fall to the ground, never to rise.

41. Be the person your creator has created you to be;
41.1. Be strong in moments and periods of adversity.
41.2. Be tough when your path passes through the Himalayas.
41.3. Moments of adversity and uphill journeys define you,
41.4. And tell your world who you are.
41.5. If you persist, you become strong.
41.6. If you fold, and give much ground to weaknesses, cut corners, bow down to gossips and other little attitudes that is it. You are defined
41.7. And if not careful, you would remain so all your life.

42. There is something beyond what the eye sees. I mentioned the name of Yashua, and doors, opportunities and thrones were made to me. I mentioned the name of Bana and doors were shut on my face.

43. The Old is the perfect child of wisdom but in the days when seasons have begun to reset, it is difficult to say if the children of wisdom would be the servants of the society.

44. Why do you say you are good to me, when you give what you do not want? Give out what is dear to you and I would sing your name.

45. The one who gives to the poor out of his plenty cannot be said to be generous, after all he demands adorations back. The one who gives out of his poverty or the little he has must be respected.

46. The Puzzle of the Titans;
46.1. China has agreed to build the "G-City."
46.2. If the Dragon fails, The Chinese brand is on the line, perhaps lost for another century.
46.3. If China builds, America has an unwinnable war on her hand.

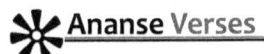 

Because Africa would not lose faith in that Dragon;

46.4. Beijing must not fail;

46.5. America must not allow.

46.6. All stand aloof looking for a way out but there is no way out.

46.7. It is I, Ananse, who devised that. It is I and no one else who knows the way out.

46.8. It is the work of my hands.

46.9. Time has determined all.

47. I know a man who abandoned his marital home to marry a wealthy and beautiful heiress. I would not do that to my wife but I would not blame that man either. I would rather pity him for having been tempted by life to make such a decision.

48. As minerals journey through the land of plants; as plant marries the animals and man is complexly seen, and journeys on, who are we not to give glory to the ELOHIM? Truly our God is a living GOD.

49. Teach me how to walk; I would learn how to run myself.

50. Good luck if you say you have finished learning, and that you do not need a teacher.

51. Learn while you are young and have the energy. A time of staleness would soon come and desire to learn would not be embraced.

52. Every young person has to be tested.

53. I mentioned the name of Ananse and every sword was pointed at my throat; I said I am a child and everyone wanted me in his home.

54. I am who I am. I would not change. I cannot change.

55. Write down your dreams and visions; expand them with time as your experiences open your horizon; review them through research and consultation with counsellors; claim them by making them your own; be prepared to stand by them no matter the circumstances, and you shall achieve them.

56. At the end of every storm, write down the lessons learnt. You would never know who would call on you for wisdom. Ananse may pop in.

57. Beware of he who sees you as the ladder to the top, once he is at the top, you would be his foot-stool.

58. Knowing what to say, is as important as how to say it and most importantly when to say it.

59. Timing is sometimes everything.

60. Carry a pen rather than a sword. I would only carry a sword when I know I am fighting fools.

61. Take note of "The She" who sees her beauty as a weapon. Once you are in her sight, you destroy her first or she runs all over you till she brings you to the ground with lifelong embarrassment and pain.

62. A person without a destination or a purpose in life is best useful when exploited or avoided at all cost.

63. Why go into battle with only one strategy. What if it doesn't work? Always have a backup plan.

64. You were in a mud as an animal would, but God's grace has lifted you up to a place of honour so that you would be to Him a son, able to reach his throne without any medium. Do not forget Him.

65. Achieving your dreams is a journey;
65.1. Beyond dreams, the euphoria, the ecstasy and joy, you would have to make time and conduct due analysis of your suitability for the dream you have so conceived for yourself. Else you would continue to dream forever.
65.2. Ask yourself, "Am I suited for the dream?"
65.3. "Do I have the basic skills to start achieving my dream?"
65.4. "Do I have the will to go through the journey?"
65.5. Oh yes, it is a journey with ups; downs, falls and getting up any time you fall.

66. Every youth has talents and, reasonably, it is appropriate to assume that, dreams should bother on your talents.

67. I have a talent. And so what? Even fools have talents. Use the talents for the common good and you would be appreciated.

## Chapter

*I am not my son.*
*My son is not me.*
*But one thing I know:*
*I trained him so well;*
*I taught him the ways of life*
*and I trained him to be a good leader.*

1. If you have no talent for something, dreaming of success in such a field would be a daunting task. It is a fool's dream. It becomes an impossibility if you are wise in your eyes enough not to learn.

2. Every dream requires a minimum amount of common-sense. Just dreaming and rumbling on is not enough. It only pleases the crowd. You would come home poor.

3. Only an ambition will not suffice. Not even Ananse can guarantee success with only an ambition. You require strength, guidance and gruesome determination.

4. Before me, it was impossible to dream and achieve a dream. After me all is possible. My happiness lies in the possibilities of these "class-one" little children who are achieving their dreams without the heavy price paid. My joy is that, we paid the price for these generations, and whether they give us credit or not is secondary. I am a happy man. When I meet Nkrumah, Jomo and Antha Diop, I would want to tell them how beautiful Mother Africa has become.

5. Bring your dreams face to face with your environment and test if the environment is suited for your dreams; otherwise, pain and tears would be your bedfellows.

6. No environment is stagnant. It changes. So should you. If the change is too slow or fast for you, pack your dreams into your bag and move to where you would be accepted.

7. Sometimes the day your dreams die is the day you die. Ananse says; "I am not ready to die."

8. When your life is at peril, every second counts; every step counts; every voice counts. In this world, your life is in perpetual peril.

9. When speaking to the wise, few words are all that is needed but to the fool, books of words would be needed; few words make him arrogant.

10. Why exaggerate your story for sympathy when sympathy only saddens your soul and weakens you.

11. Pain only becomes worse if you give him notice. He is already here so move on.

12. There comes a time when threats only delay you and make the situation worse. Act!

13. How can you defeat your enemies if you do not know your weaknesses? You think they are idle? A competent adversary knows his enemy through and through. They know you.

14. If you eat the voices in these Verses and they sound good in your mouths, hearts and minds, know that they came at a great cost to Ananse.

15. Well, opportunities do not matter if they are not utilized for good.

16. There are times to take risks and times to simply move on.

17. Who says talent is everything? What about training, the environment, opportunities and motivation? Know all. Appreciate the full picture and you would be fulfilled.

18. Not all good decisions end up in comfort. Some end up making your situation worse but be proud you made them.

19. Be honest with yourself before you start believing the lies you are telling the society and being trapped.

20. Which of the voices is the voice of God? Is it the incoherent one asking me to believe in myself, and look within for salvation or the one pointing me to a great mountain of gold and flesh or the one pointing to a human saviour residing in a temple of marble and granite?

21. Misfortune happens to everyone. Do not laugh at my misfortune. Do not despise me. Do not regard yourself as wiser. Misfortune would fall on you when he is ready and I would be there to ask you why. Be wise and be humble.

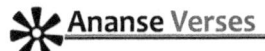 

22. The wise prepares for days of trouble but the fool gallops on as if life is only a matter of a day and a step.

23. If you have a career, love it; yearn for it and grow in it.

24. There is always a point of reality in all endeavours. Even dreamers wake up.

25. Do not dream forever; do not hope forever. A time comes when you have to wake up.

26. Respond to this tent of flesh, giving you shelter in a chaos world else your soul wanders and finds no home. Remember to keep the balance. Remember to keep the soul in control for no flesh exists in the kingdom of God.

27. Let the trained psychologist be counsellor; let the software developer write programmes. Let the teacher, teach. In this manner, we shall utilise our strengths and honour our societies appropriately with our skill. In this lies progress and prosperity.

28. In the real world of today, never leave anything to chance for chance is no friend to a lazy man.

29. Small issues matter, big issues matter. How beautiful the world is if both come together to prominence.

30. Who says you need a billion to start a business worth billions? All you need is an idea, the attitude, and a Cedi (GHC1.00).

31. Train your eyes; train your ears; train your body; be cold for the world is cold.

32. You are free not because chains have been removed from your wrist. Your freedom stems from gaining your mind from deception, lies and dogmas. You are free because your mind is free from chains of customs and traditions.

33. In the end, it is all about being a good citizen, a good father, having love in your heart and living in peace with Mother earth and yourself. Whatever follows or the consequence of your love, take it as part of a divine plan.

34. I was happy when I scored a 90% and passed but I was disturbed when I heard that my brother had also passed even though with a 41%.

35. Always remember your enemies. Know their thoughts. Know their inclinations and strive to understand them. In this knowledge lies life.

# Chapter

*Live and let us live. Die and let us live....*
*To die or to live depends on the will of MAN.*
*God is forever a benevolent Judge.*

1. Patience is a rare virtue, which even the wise finds difficult to master.

2. Are you ready?

3. Ananse asks, "Mr President, do you think the people would worry if you fly to Abuja for breakfast, Accra for lunch and Khartoum for dinner and sleep in Kigali?" Ananse responds, "No, they would not as long as you provide them with housing, security, food, and toilets as the book people would say, "Basic amenities." But since you have failed, even the glass of water you drink has become a subject of jealousy and contention.

4. This is simply the time for accountability. Why do you run for cover? If you did well, you would meet the masses with open arms but here you are, hiding in a hole.

5. Know that real security does not come from material wealth. In the moment of truth it would flee, leaving you to wane and dry into lifelong shame.

6. If my body is the temple of God, why should I be worried about what I wear or eat when what matters is my thoughts. Well, worry about everything if what you eat causes your thoughts to wonder on filth or what you wear tempts a weaker soul beyond what he could bear.

7. How far can you run from your sins; how fast can you run from your deeds O runner. When you decide you have run from all your sins and feel safe to rest, you would only find out you have taken rest on the seat of Accountability.

8. Finally, be sure of yourself and note that, you cannot do more than your abilities would allow you to.

9. You can fatten the calf but no matter how much you try, it can never be as big as the elephant.

10. Take time to arrive at a decision. When it is done, follow through with it. Never abandon it. Look to the left or right only to improve the decision.

11. Talents and skills are the obvious bedrock for your dreams and career springboard.

12. For talents to bear meaningful fruits, they ought to be nurtured, developed, and guided.

13. Your best salesmen are your talents, potentials, and skills.

14. When chosen leaders leave God with no choice, He hands the nation over to the devil.

15. When a nation lusts for deception, they choose evil men as their leaders. Their ears are eager for tales of ecstasy and so they are swept off.

16. Motivation is a fountain of energy.

17. The Hour is here with us;
17.1. A time was on the horizon.
17.2. That hour is here that; no longer would Mother Africa allow her children to be abused and slaughtered nor would she allow the older children sell her young into slavery for pleasure or out of folly.
17.3. She has risen to defend her lands;
17.4. And to protect her children with her last breadth.
17.5. With the fire from the bellies of the assailants of her children, she would slaughter them and bring freedom to her children.

18. Drive is an inner force which keeps you going irrespective of physical constraints. It helps you to manoeuvre emotional constraints. Drive impels you to focus and commit to your dreams. Without drive, you lose much of your edge, energy and motivation.

19. "You cannot solve long term challenges with short term solutions", Ananse said that for children to sing. What Ananse did not add was that, "It takes wisdom to identify whether the challenges are long term or short term."

20. Preparation is everything. It is a perfect companion in all endeavours. Preparation equips you with the skills, resources and abilities needed for the goals set.

21. Mental preparation is the sacred oil, which burns to mesh all skills in perfect harmony beneath the physical frame. It is reflected by right attitude, conviction, and possession of core values, toughness, perseverance, readiness, enthusiasm and the desire to learn and grow.

22. Dreams are sometimes like mirages;
22.1. They turn beggars into kings, slaves into masters and the homeless into estate owners.
22.2. In the dream world, everything is smooth and harmonious.
22.3. There are neither tears nor sorrows.
22.4. It is a world of perpetual bliss.
22.5. A world of abundance, where there is neither scarcity nor disappointment.

23. Say to your body and soul, "All is well."

24. In the mind of the optimist, peace and happiness reigns. In the mind of the pessimist, peace and happiness are rare occurrences. The pessimist sees darkness more often and labour every morning. At daybreak he laughs at fortune; at sunset, he counts only what he holds and upon it, he allows himself a fleeting smile of the pessimist he is.

25. Sometimes, all it takes to redeem yourself is to say, "I am sorry."

26. The warrior conquers with pleasure and pain in his heart. He is filled with pleasure because he is a warrior with victories under his belt; he bears pain in his heart because he knows that with a swing from another warrior, he would be like those he has sent beyond the river. Yet he holds no grudges; he holds no complaints. He only holds his badge of ascension in his heart and on his forehead, knowing that his life is to a purpose.

27. Watch your steps; guard your heart and tread calmly, for great-

ness is only a step away from fall or so; a fall is a step away from greatness. So is wisdom a step away from folly. One misstep and you are in a whirlwind. This is the great reality God has placed in nature to protect man from being what he would say in his heart he is when he dines with the divine.

28. Kingdoms, Flesh, Blood and Water and Earth;
28.1. We are beyond flesh and blood.
28.2. For a long time we have been here.
28.3. Contenting with forces that roll in strange worlds with their strange elements.
28.4. Their kingdoms invisible to our material realms.
28.5. It is time to pray.
28.6. Who does not know the great evil of this planet?
28.7. But who can shout it?
28.8. I say it is time to pray.
28.9. When there is war, you know who is behind;
28.10. When fire erupts, we know who set it off;
28.11. When blood flows in the streets, you know who spills it;
28.12. It is time to fight this evil with divine weapons.
28.13. Let us dedicate our lands to the God of heaven.
28.14. Let us say to Him, "Come and take your home in our midst. Dwell among us; be our God and we shall be your people. Guide us to build our nations once again. And teach us to protect ourselves."
28.15. O LORD, we pray.

29. Man, know that much of creation owes her living to Mother Africa. But she is silent at the abuse of her children.

30. Why does the wise always run from leadership but the fool always gallops for it? Know that, leadership is a backbreaking burden. Do not yearn for it. Do not go for it when not chosen. If you fail God's children, a great disaster awaits you.

31. Surely, the day of accountability will come. It is unavoidable. So those who have been given so much, be prepared.

32. Within the bliss of good conscience, you have hope, purpose

and light to guide you as you pertain to the ideals of your lofty humanity.

33. Why are leaders of men so difficult to understand? The people have no need of your luxury, palaces or appetites. They only require a home, and two square meals yet you deny them? And in their hunger, they rise and deny you our palaces and luxuries!

34. How do you intend to prevent strife and bloodshed by the masses when the society is controlled by only a few, when the masses have no route to fulfilment?

35. Sometimes it is not what is said which matters but what is held back.

36. If you failed with plenty, do you think you can succeed with nothing? Seek wisdom and all shall be well.

37. Bold dreams are the ones that leave your footprints in history.

38. "No dream is too big to be achieved." "As long as your mind can conceive it, it can be achieved." Ananse did not say this. Someone wiser did.

39. Is there a difference between the fool and a madman? The fool touches what he is supposed not to touch; tastes what he is supposed not to even smell; sees what he is supposed not to and dreams of dining with the devil. The madman knows no difference among these.

40. Nothing is impossible. The only thing impossible is for change to cease its cycles.

41. The child feeds on dreams but the wise grows the dreams into reality, thereby bringing fulfilment to a troubled soul.

42. Let your dreams serve you as guidelines in your psychological compass as you navigate through the harsh realities of life.

43. You need to dream of a society better for all and work to achieve it. For your peace and comfort is nurtured and grown in the sharing among all.

44. I have seen Love conquer all but then many wise men have chosen Peace over Love. As for Ananse, he made no decision. He merely allowed this life to take its course. And it was love. But on hindsight, he says it was a mistake. A fatal error. He should have chosen peace as the wise always do. God's planet is too corrupt a place to wish for a holy grail such as love. To ask for love on this planet is to ask for so much from The ELOHIM.

45. Would financial status and temporal power matter in a society where a man is measured by the highest moral values?

46. How lucky are those who wish to live a modest life: a decent house, a wife, a husband, a family and three square meals a day. They would save themselves from the unbearable burdens of grand ambition, which has enslaved many a poor soul and led a manifold to inflict themselves with mortal wounds.

47. Why do you dream when you have not cultivated boldness, courage, single-mindedness, perseverance, endurance, firmness and steady-mindedness? Dreams alone do not survive in the real world.

48. Without the right attitudes and balance, your dreams would not grow beyond your nose and ego.

# Chapter

*Have pity on those trapped by their ambitions.*
*Slaves are better off.*

1. Dreams and reality are not friends but always go hand in hand. Sometimes you get more than you dreamt for and at other times you get less.

2. We are on the way up but we are not there yet. The good news is that, we are on the right path. Our hope is that, we shall get there.

3. Dreams should be the inspirational roadmap of your life's ambition; a motivator and a silent voice in the storms of life; a friend adding purpose and energy to your life.

4. Marriage matters to Mother Africa. Marriage matters to mother Earth. Marriage is the web by which society finds its soul of unity and care for one another.

5. Are you really bold? You speak your mind and say it as you want to. Would you speak your mind if you knew that what you say could cost you your life, or hurt someone you love?

6. Dream neither despairs nor accepts the failures of life. It is a platform for miracles and impossibilities; a friend who drives away fear, despair, failure and positions you always in the right light for you to receive success and fulfilment at the right times. What a companion!

7. Know when to stop and you would be a happy man.

8. Wake up Princes and Princesses and take your palaces of honour. Mother AFRICA is calling.

9. Do you know why we say Mother Africa? She is the noblest and eldest Mother of all.

10. Everything they have is a carbon copy... look for the original.

11. He said; give me 77 tons of gold and I would make an exact copy of the Azieze. But the wise one said; give him 7 tons of clay and let us see what he can do with it first.

12. Pray for failure when you know your success lies in that failure. At that point, the concept of failure becomes simply an illusion.

13. Peace is Priceless.

14. How big can the antelope grow? Can he be like the Cow? Dream no evil; touch not the arrogance of perverted minds nor their guiles; for all would stand accountable before the God of All Hosts.

15. Think of the day. The future belongs to the future.

16. Love has 667 dimensions. The human mind can only accommodate 117. Of these; he has the vocabulary to explain only 21. Even then, the teacher is willing to teach only 7.

17. From one, you go to two; from two you go to three; from three you go to four; why jump from one to four?

18. Be yourself. There is no one like you. Why try to be someone you are not?

19. True friendship is Priceless.

20. We need some leaders to lead and guide us to the top. We need others to keep us at the top, and we need others to lead us to downfall to complete the cycle all societies must abide by.

## Chapter

*If you choose to go with the multitude on the common and easy path, you are likely to be as common as the path you have taken.*

1. Are you afraid to take risks? No one would remember your name.

2. The words of the pauper, "I knew you. I knew Kofi Annan too. I even bought food for him and paid his rents."

3. Some get home by car, others by train, and others by boat, and others on foot. Whatever the means, we all get home.

4. All the energy you need is that required for the first step. Just take the first step.

5. In a war no one wins but war. War then is the enemy of humanity.

6. Ask yourself, "What skills do I need in order to achieve my dreams?" Because as has been echoed over and over again, dreams without skills are like the empty rhetoric of a cunning politician.

7. Ananse says, "The madness of politics is difficult to explain to the masses. More so, when the masses is everything that matters but do not know it." Ananse says, "Policies alone do not win elections. It takes a bit of deceit, blackmail, slander, thuggery and an elaborate dose of illusions. That is why, like the mother Church, thieves, thugs, fast speakers and priests are critical to every political machine. Policies do not win elections. Politics does. You, who aspire for public office, consider and learn."

8. How do I acquire the skills and resources required to achieve my dreams when I am in a valley? Ananse says, "Fight your way up. Do not accept "no" to your dreams. Do not accept the status quo's definition of your life."

9. Know thy enemy. By knowing your enemy, the battle is within victory's reach. It is only by knowing your enemy that you can strategise and plan for victory.

10. Do not accept all that is said. Ask questions; probe to learn and you would find what you are looking for and more.

11. Approach life with an open mind; embrace pain and challenges with an open mind and you would just find out that they are necessary companions of human life. Put them in the proper box at the right energy level and you would be just fine.

12. Entrenched positions, stereotypes and fixed views only make you narrow, and limit your opportunities. Open your mind and you would know how wonderful the horizon is.

13. Sometimes, all that is needed is to wait! So the wise talks about patience.

14. Remember to remember what is to be remembered. A momentary slip and a great opportunity is lost. Remember what is to be remembered at the right time and you would be welcomed and loved.

15. I have my priorities; you have yours; note that, you are never my Number 1 priority as I am not to you. You are only Number 1 on your priority considerations. So do not count on me to save you. If you cannot save yourself, then you are doomed.

16. Some thoughts are best kept in the mind. Others in the heart; others should never be kept at all. You let them pass through your mind as soon as they enter it; for in letting them go lies life, happiness and comfort.

17. Keep moving forward. There is no reward in looking back when you are running towards your goals. Keep moving till you come to the place of cycles.

18. Work hard towards achieving your dreams... that is all that matters. That is what you would be remembered for. That is what would give you satisfaction and fulfilment.

19. All counsel is more of guidelines than rules. Make the most of them if you deem them helpful to your life.

20. Attaining one's dreams go beyond poetry, colourful language and excitement. It rests on sound wisdom and pragmatism. It includes a lot of guidance.

21. Sometimes you learn from associations. At other times, you learn from the streets through shocks, failures, tears and groans.

22. There is wisdom in understanding that, to achieve your dreams, you need other people's collective knowledge, experiences, wisdom and resources.

23. My father told me, "My son, note that every person you meet is important in your cumulative collection of wisdom, skills and learning. Ananse says, "Respect everyone you meet. Young, old, white, red, or yellow."

24. The lures of daydreaming are enticing. They have the attractiveness to hold you, even as you see them as fantasies and waste all your most precious resource; Time. So beware of daydreaming.

25. Be reminded that you are continually required to learn and employ the knowledge to develop yourself in order to move to the next level.

26. Learning and patience are success factors.

27. Your current challenges are only a bad storm; contain them and hold your trials in dignity. How else could you call yourself a man? There are others out there who are in worse situations.

28. When there is no precedent to what is to be done, create your own path. Do not throw your arms up in resignation.

29. When the status quo does not allow new ideas or dreams to be nurtured and be realised, fight it.

30. Honour, duty and pain.

     *A tribute to the invisible stars who keep us all safe day and night; soldiers in the endless war of creating, building and sustaining a better society; You are our reliable shield.*

30.1. The world we are creating would be so pure that when it is completed, there would be no place in it for us;.

30.2. Yes, we, the creators, would have no place in the society because we would be unfit to live in it.

30.3. We shall only stare at it from afar.

30.4. This is not the result of our innate impurity, but it is because our hands would be sullied in the building process.

30.5. What a high but necessary price to pay

30.6. This is our duty.

30.7. We shall be glad to have built that city when the world flocks to have a glimpse of the gold city.

30.8. This is our honour.

30.9. History would judge us harshly.

30.10. Little children would sit in the comfort and security of the world we have created, eat from the silver plates we have placed in their hands and be masters to pass judgement on our deeds.

30.11. This is our pain.

30.12. The worlds we protect hates us, despise us and denounce our methods. Methods we know no other;

30.13. And the society shouts with hilarious joy at our fall.

30.14. Liberty, freedom, individual rights, rule of law...have won the day, hurray!

30.15. We soldier on. This is our pledge and we are men of honour!

30.16. We do not seek solace from the adulations of children or some benign masses.

30.17. We have found inspiration from our pledge to duty.

30.18. We are soldiers.

31. We all have divinity and evil in us. It is all about divine choice, divine plan, divine designs, genetics, the environment and above all choice.

32. I am a slave today because I have not made any choice. One thing I am certain of is that tomorrow I would be a free man. I slave myself today to buy myself out of poverty and slavery. This is my choice. This is the path I have chosen to freedom.

I would not be a master tomorrow because I seek that not. All I seek is the freedom. This is my choice.

# Chapter

*God gave truth to man.*
*Man turned the truth into a weapon,*
*Not to defend the truth but to attack the truth*
*So that the masses would continue to be in slavery.*
*Is it the error of God or the test of God?*

1. Good fortune and chance would only smile on you favourably if they see you in warm embrace with planning, hard work and determination.

2. Plan the hour, plan the day, plan the day after, plan forever.

3. Are you comfortable that you eat and drink without working for it? This is neither the way of honour nor dignity. Toil for your bread and when you have succeeded, you would lift your head high and take your seat at the gate among men. Then you would be proud when your children call you Father and your wife, my Husband because you have earned it.

4. It takes a long time to identify the best route to create and choose a career. Within that period, you would see failure, betrayals and deceptions. But as a man and son of God, your good intentions would shield your soul and the failures would harden and give you passage through rocky places.

5. In the face of opposition create your own path. That is the way of the Eagle. Chicken would cock and hide. Parrots would imitate and take the frequently travelled road.

6. Freedom is expensive.

7. The nation requires the tomato sellers to sell to us. So are the farmers to feed us and the seamstresses to clothe us. They are doing pretty good jobs for us. How diligent they are! How diligent the little man is! What of those in higher places who have chosen to be our eyes, ears and brains. Clearly, they are refusing to think for us. They see smoke and hear ghost whispers day and night. They have forgotten their duties.

8. When a man knows what is right and chooses the wrong path, words alone would not be enough to turn him away from the wrong path.

9. Ananse dares say that, "Do not despise the one upon whose work you stand as a foundation. He might bring you down. After all he is a man, and not God, to understand your nuances and forgive."

10. There is always a period of rest. It comes with achievement, wisdom and conclusion;

10.1. A time the body needs to regenerate, and the soul to search and fulfil.

10.2. There is always an end.

10.3. You have reached here having achieved your dreams or having missed opportunities.

10.4. There are those who reach this stage having achieved their dreams to the fullest or having had their dreams truncated by the harsh realities of life, with no more strength left to fight on.

10.5. There is no room for redress at this stage.

10.6. Ananse says "whatever your lot count your achievements and blessings and say goodbye."

10.7. Be content and you would find that rare happiness which comes to only a few.

10.8. Resist and fight on and you would destroy all your footprints.

10.9. What is important to know is that you accept the end of your journey in the spirit of contentment.

10.10. If you grumble, you poison the whole dough.

11. Stress and headache, which one comes first? I do not know. What I know is, both are enemies of good health.

12. When you see your end, do not struggle like a desperate child or cry like a baby; meet it with smiles and go in dignity.

13. When you cross roads with bitterness, anger and restlessness, simply do the sensible thing; buy patience and retrace your steps, else you would sleep on a bed of tragedy.

14. Ill-fate and misfortune are born into our lives every day but the wise always overcome them.

15. Some achieve what they set out to achieve; others achieve more than what they set out for; others fail to reach their own marks. Whatever your lot, when your strength is gone, whatever you have achieved, gladly accept it and give gratitude to God.

Why worry yourself to a painful old age when there is not much you could do?

16. Follow the path of truth and you would live in peace and harmony with your conscience. There would be no fear of anything haunting you. You would be at peace with yourself, society and with God, your Creator. What more do you want?

17. Whatever you have, say to yourself: "I am the happiest man on earth," for you do not know the hell all the wealth of the earth would bring you.

18. No one should judge a man for what he does to survive and to take care of his family, except God.

19. This world is set in laws and keys. You find them, you are a creator of worlds and happiness: You ignore them, you are a slave; only doors of gloom and tears would be opened to you.

20. Ambition, common sense, and reality are all independent worlds but if they fail to find a common ground for them to work together, they become time bombs.

21. Dreamlands: "This period is beyond the fulfilment. You have gone beyond fulfilment and you are at a level you never knew of, never dreamt of and so did not wish for. This is the final dream. The subconscious dreams of a child at seven have been realised and gone beyond. The pure dreams of childhood have survived the turmoil of this life to come face to face with reality and have conquered. Those who reach this stage usually say, "I never thought I would be here. This is more than I asked for. It is a time of bliss and humility."

22. O how sweet, romantic, and soothing fulfilment it would be. Ananse says at that point, "You have no care for money, fame, or power. You are above the pull and tug of the flesh. You have come to see the fruitlessness of money, temporal power and self-seeking ambitions. You are in the circle of Noblemen. You have become a watcher of the affairs of men; laughing at the

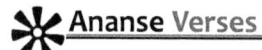 

needless squabbles of men struggling to rise and conquer the world."

23. Pursue not fame, money or the adulations of the world or their airs; they are all deceptions...vanity. Do not take their blood covenants. They are shadows. Pursue the true light of God and you would preserve the divine plan.

24. "Jam the path with obstacles and the children would miss the path. Bring hailstorm of troubles on them and the children would sell their souls cheap." This has been the age-old modus of leaders of men. Look to God when you face brick walls. Look within when all seem lost.

25. The blessings of the Old age,
At the dawn of grey hair, the old man has become an encyclo-paedia of wisdom and knowledge. You are a prophet. You could look at a person and tell where the path he has taken would end. You have become a form of a god entrusted with the fore-sight of seers. If properly fed, she would bless the society with her wisdom and from that fountain, we shall drink the waters of life and prosperity.

26. I am the greatest in my family. I am the greatest in my village. I am the greatest in the nation. I am among the world's great-est. I am the greatest among the greatest. Ananse says, "All are great" in their respective worlds.

27. Beauty can tame the madman. It can heal the sick and set the lost to the path of God or set the virtuous to the fold of perdi-tion. Beauty is a medicine. Beauty is a weapon, for good or for ill.

28. There are those, and they are many, who see religion as a weap-on to their material ends and not as a means to spiritual rebirth and or growth. These are the true evil we must conquer.

29. Those of us Mother Earth has blessed with her dew and milk are merely keepers. Rich man, wealthy individual, a millionaire or a billionaire, we are just keepers. We are keeping the wealth for

God's other children, to feed, provide for and protect them. You are merely a Keeper. The moment you claim it as your own, all around you begin to live in hunger and poverty. O Keeper, you have betrayed a sacred trust entrusted to you by Mother Earth.

30. You crave for Peace. You seek fulfilment and harmony so you have conquered perseverance. You have sought Wisdom and found him. You have sought for Knowledge and met her. Have you finally conquered Patience? She is a bit tricky. Wait till you conquer her.

31. There are those who dream to conquer the world and achieve it through bursts of madness, tears, wars and defeats; they set their tables at the foot of God. It is within this that they are fulfilled.

32. World Icons. O how we sing their greatness and in it we find pleasure and pride. By it we encourage a whole nation to dream. Through their feats a whole nation is inspired. Have we understood the price they paid?

33. The Mysteries of this world, they say, are right under our noses. How do we find them?

34. Space and galactic travels would one day, very soon, be as common as hopping from Accra to Lagos. Yes, the time is even here with us. It would overtake us like a storm and all truth would be made bare. And gods would be messengers. Their empires of pain and hunger would become ruins because a new world would be born- a world they did not create; a world they do not have the keys to enter. Then from afar, God's children would look at them scrambling for shelter and say, "This is how low the LORD has brought those who tormented us." And we would rejoice in our new world free, protected, and blessed.

35. Watch your words; choose them carefully, let your mind follow it encoding through its delivery. For you would never know where else those words would end up. Yes, there is always someone listening.

36. Last words. Do I know all that I have written? I do not. Do I understand all that I have written? Much of it I do not. They came by words of knowledge, discernment, wisdom and hearing. So when I seal this phase, the next time I pick "The Ananse Verses" to read, I would do so as a student.

37. In the end, the best to ever happen to you is to hold nothing. In that nothingness, the flesh has no hold on you and you are free to face the truth and embrace freedom.

38. Divine MAN. The human being, when blessed by The Elohim, is taught to heal by touch, breadth or even by the words of his mouth. It is not a miracle; it is Man being ONE with his Maker and being blessed to ascend to the heights he truly ought to be.

# Chapter

*In a game of Chess, if you hear "checkmate",*
*do not disrupt the game.*
*Be a sportsman;*
*accept your position and play your best move;*
*There is always another game to play.*

1.  Stick to what you know. The good you seek would always find a way to meet you. Take progressive steps and never fly into the air because you could. Do not embark on an adventure of fools and restless souls.

2.  Know your strengths, develop them, and they would bring you success and joy. Can you compete with Albert Einstein in the field of Physics? So why do you want to be him when you can teach him how to write a love letter? Being you is the key to fulfilment. Being like someone is the key to failure.

3.  I have asked. I have believed. Now I am receiving because I asked with a humble heart and believed with faith.

4.  Greatness is not by chance. You have to work for it. You have to achieve it. You would have to pay the price for it;

    4.1.  Ananse says he learnt to speak; he learnt to listen; he learnt to observe; he learnt to wash his hands.

    4.2.  He learnt the art of silence; he also learnt which words to speak, how to say them, and when to say them.

    4.3.  Above all, he had a good conscience and the best of intentions so even when he was betrayed by his youthfulness, he was vindicated by his clear conscience. Because when the elders sit down to judge him, they always found out that his errors were without wickedness or malice and with this, his errors would not be counted against him.

    4.4.  Can a young person come close to the elders, and stay by them without erring?

5.  You who think you are "wise" and crave to put fools in position of influence to manipulate them, Ananse says beware. The fool is a double-edged sword. He could be a tool for you and against you. Prepare for your nightmare if your puppets fall into the hands of other "wise" men.

6.  Talent is to be used for good. If you see your talent as a means to wealth or to fame, that is not God's work. That is vanity.

7.  Every government has the capacity to pick people from the

streets, give them hope and turn them into pillars of society. If a government rather breaks her citizens up, then that government has no legitimacy. The leaders do not have the blessings of the Most High. These are Ananse's proposals;

7.1. First of all, assemble the cronies around that government and take them on a merry ride.

7.2. When any member of that government falls sick, take him to the in-country hospitals they have built for the people.

7.3. When they are thirsty, give them the water from the public water system; if none exists, let them drink from the nearest source of water.

7.4. Do not accept their gifts because they would twist your tongue and corrupt your judgement.

7.5. Do not eat their food because it would poison your body and stain your inner sanctuary.

7.6. Do not mention their names when you are in a good mood. God would be angry with you if you do.

7.7. Do not mention their names in your songs.

7.8. Purge their eyes from among your midst.

7.9. Pull out the tongues of their voices.

7.10. And say a prayer for the nation because when what must be done is done, you would need the hand of the LORD in healing the wounds therefrom.

8. I confess my sins to God and ask for His grace to overcome my weakness. I leave my path to Him. In Him do I commit myself, and I am assured of salvation. Why should I commit my path to man who is there today but no more tomorrow?

9. I pitch my tent in the house of God so that He would build his glorious Kingdom in me. For I am dust and ashes. I am only a corrupted mortal. But if I could free myself from this flesh, then I would be truly free and honoured. Then I would be indestructible because I would dwell in the house of God all my life.

10. Beware of Him who can destroy your body and soul. Beware of them that claim to have learnt His ways and have had a glimpse of it. Beware of them that have lost it all and have nothing to lose.

11. The tyrant must not die now. If we remove him now, there would be no better person to take his place and there would be anarchy. The tyrant must not die now. If we cut him now, a more evil man would replace him and we will be worse off. Let us be wise. Ananse says, "Let us prepare a benevolent replacement in silence, then, when we have tested him to be true, we can remove the tyrant."

12. My son, I leave you with these boxes of gold and other precious minerals. They are not for you but your children. They are not for your children but for their children; they are not for your children's children but for their children. The wise son would always leave for his children more than he inherited, even if he inherited nothing.

13. Remember to remember to leave enough for all who come after you. They deserve a share of God's resources. And they would bless you if you do. That would make your journey to our fathers smoother.

14. Share with the needy. Share even in poverty.

15. When you are at the top and all your wishes can be honoured, how can you survive the laws of the Most High God to be humble and love your poor neighbour?

16. Do you know that dreams come with sacrifices? Do you know that, they have costs and that even if The Sovereign LORD whispers your future to you; you still have to pay the price? Everybody pays the price.

17. When the hunter becomes the hunted and the hunted becomes the hunter, then know that the time of liberation has come; freedom has come to those once enslaved.

18. The knowledge of your kind, the knowledge of yourself, and knowledge of your origin is the only true knowledge. With this knowledge, no one can take your future from you.

19. We are here in this mess, yes in this mud. We are where we are today because once our leaders get into office, they turn their

backs on society. Once they get into office, their preoccupation becomes the perfecting of weapons of looting the nation. Fat animals. How roasting them would be easier because their fat would embolden the fires of the roasting piles.

20. Because we succeeded, we were respected. All our friends came back. Even our enemies give us respect. Rise and embrace success.

21. Time is an illusion which God has placed on man as an eternal limitation to remind us of our mortality and boundaries. So that foolish mortal shall not claim the thrones of eternity.

22. Let us treat our women with respect. Without them our seeds bear no fruit; without them our children grow without education; without them we are lost.

23. The future of every society is tied to the quality of her youth. Ananse says, "A nation is made strong by her citizens."

24. Some goals could only be achieved through patience.

25. Many of you have long lost your sparkle in the face of unguided dreams and ambitions, which were neither rooted in reality nor common sense. Remember the words of Eno; remember the echoes of her voice returning to you from afar with salt. Ananse says, "Dream but take counsel and refresh the dreams as the world keeps changing around you. Let time be your eternal guide.

26. Life is a journey requiring thought, guidance, planning, sacrifices, balance and strength.

27. The deeper you dig, even though the more you bear, the closer you come to your goal.

28. Continue to pray; continue to hope; continue to hope, for you do not know the hour deliverance would announce itself at your door. Always be prepared.

29. You need the right environment in order to achieve your

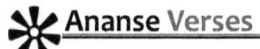 

dreams. YES, the right environment. Ananse cannot be wrong on this.

30. The race of front liners, challengers and losers:
30.1. In a race, the front-runner becomes desperate when the challenger catches up with him.
30.2. This is where the battle is toughest and dirtiest.
30.3. This is when both dig up;
30.4. The one who perseveres long enough wins.
30.5. If the front-runner looks over his shoulder, he loses out,
30.6. If the challenger looks at the face of the front-runner, he also loses out.
30.7. He who would look at the goal as within reach and grinds ahead would be the winner.

31. A code of War: "Gladly face the challenger that opens up his intention and fights you in the open. But the one who hides in the shadows, lurks in darkness waiting for you to slip, seek him, bloody him out and make him an example to all saboteurs."

32. Some errors when you commit them, you would survive; but these two are never to be done: never make a child a leader and never leave power on the laps of someone who has not earned it nor tested.

33. Do not deny your humanity. Do not deny your African root. Do not deny your skin. You are beautifully made and created to reflect the will of God. Those who deny themselves would be lost in the vast expanse of creation with neither a home to call their own nor a family to claim them.

34. There is always someone to sell out; there is always a weak link; you only have to look harder.

35. "I see Africa rising. I see an Africa contributing 60% of world trade. An Africa where one day skyscrapers would adorn our skylines, with our own global brands across our continent." Yes, Ananse agrees with the dreamer but he asks, "Does Af-

rica believe in such a dream?" Know that, *Believing is every-thing.*

36.    Cautions and pronouncements;
36.1.  Every corrupt politician is a curse, run from him,
36.2.  Every leader who takes his quota but denies the people their iota is cursed right to his seventh generation of children and family,
36.3.  Every leader who does not put the people first is an abomination to his family and community,
36.4.  May he be cursed and punished? Definitely.
36.5.  May their misfortunes far exceed the cries of the people.
36.6.  May their stolen wealth become a nightmare to them;
36.7.  May the food in their mouths turn into ashes;
36.8.  May they or their children never know peace as long as someone goes to bed on an empty stomach in the society as a result of their actions.
36.9.  May every man of the clergy who refuses to see nor caution them be counted among their evil.
36.10. And may they also come to a worse fate.

37.    "Many of our early battles are lost but the War is not lost. It would never be lost. And never again would our people be exploited." Can our African leaders, professionals, business leaders, the clergy and intelligentsia make a solemn pledge to a "never again creed?"

38.    Do not be filled with bitterness. Do not be a friend to those enamoured by it. Draw your energy from Love. If you do, you would survive whatever is thrown at you.

39.    As a youth of the world, if you have lost hope, dream again. Set your horizon high, for you have what it takes to achieve your dreams.

# Chapter

*No one would build your house for you.*
*Dream again..*
*...Build your lands.*
*Build your infrastructures;*
*Stop this senseless materialism;*
*Love your youth.*
*O Africa.*

1. The sceptre of God:
1.1. Be grateful for the future;
1.2. Be grateful for the present;
1.3. Be grateful for the past;
1.4. Be grateful for the pain, tears and joys.
1.5. They are all laden with gold nuggets.
1.6. Be grateful for everyone;
1.7. Be grateful for everything.

2. Ananse says, "I lose my voice and wisdom in the presence of divine wisdom, so I listen and eat my full."

3. Do not stand by the streets and look out for trouble. It is a fool's venture. But when trouble finds you herself, do not skirt; do not fret; face it like a man because it is in that challenge that you would earn wisdom which no amount of reading of books would bestow.

4. What you cherish and love in your heart is the source of your happiness or misfortune. It is all by divine design coded in our genes as mortals.

5. Very soon, that time is even here when holy men shall sanction divorce in the Church and the society would applaud and God in Heaven would consider;
5.1. Yes, very soon, "what God has joined, let no one put asunder..." would be obliterated.
5.2. Well, did God put you together or you schemed to get him to marry you.
5.3. Maybe you blackmailed him;
5.4. Maybe you deceived him with a false pregnancy;
5.5. Maybe you bought his silence;
5.6. Maybe you raped her; O yes, she had no option. She was bound in chains and handed over;
5.7. Many a man or woman is trapped in marriage.
5.8. The beautiful institution has become an eternal prison to many.
5.9. Every day they groan for freedom.

5.10. Every hour they yearn for a delivery.

5.11. Perhaps a time would come when death would be the major player.

6. A master has the moral uprightness, conviction, vision, simplicity and the courage to attract lesser leaders to follow his calling;

6.1. Through his inspiration, he rallies the masses to a cause greater than himself.

6.2. In addition, long after he is gone, the fire would continue to burn.

6.3. He builds his civilization not on the strength of man but on a spiritual light that forever shines.

6.4. He creates a land where everyone shares in that great light of liberty, security, fulfillment and rest.

6.5. His message is not the deception of or for material gain or the vain accolades of vanity. It is something greater. Something lasting. Something far loftier and graceful.

6.6. His values come forth from the throne of God to shed light in a dark world of pain and desolation.

6.7. It creates a world where hunger for the material is disgraced and defeated.

7. This world is an ecosystem of eternal wars and battles. Savour your brief moments of joy. For very soon another battle would begin. Yes, hardly would you grasp a victory than another begins. In all our affairs, let us remember Him who created us and His laws for our peace and victories.

8. The only "Knowing", which you should know, is knowing what to know and knowing what not to know. And if you were able to know this, you would truly be a wise person, able to guide the path of multitudes to safety, prosperity and happiness

9. There are "somethings" you would be told; others, you would surely come to know but the most important ones you must find out yourself.

10. Let them underrate you. Let the people say all that they can but do not underrate yourself nor believe what they say about you. In the end, it is only about you.

11. The great song of humanity:
11.1. We all have our roles; we all play our roles.
11.2. In each role lies a chord,
11.3. In our combined chords lay hidden a harmony,
11.4. In our combined roles would a harmony be born,
11.5. In our interactions lies a great song,
11.6. Songs of liberation, purpose, glory and creation; each selected by the maker,
11.7. Each trained by THE MOST HIGH,
11.8. Each set to play by LORD GOD ALMIGHTY,
11.9. All created by THE ELOHIM
11.10. O how beautiful our song would be if we shall know our roles and play our tunes accordingly,
11.11. What a great song we shall sing if a master is born to us to guide us in playing our parts.

12. When you are floating in the vast expanse of life, you always need a point of reference.

13. The bomb would definitely be dropped. You knew that when you crossed the line. Yes, the decision was made when you made the decision to cross the line. There is no time for mercy. This is justice. Brace yourself, a command has been given, the weapons are armed, here comes the hailstorm.

14. Of all the beauty, which the eye has seen, is any of them greater than these: love, light and beauty?

15. It pays to listen to the educated woman. After all she is as educated as you are and has seen much of life as you. Who says she is second to you? The society?

16. In your quiet moments, pray thus: "I thank God for my life. I am grateful for the food I eat, the water I drink and the health I enjoy and the air I breathe. Gratitude is the price of abundance."

17. Set yourself free to enslave yourself; enslave yourself to set yourself free; slavery or freedom, does it matter in the land? It all exists in your mind.

18. "You are wise, teacher", the student said. The teacher responded, "Yes, I am as wise as God empowers me to. The rest, I am only a learned person who through pains, sacrifices and tears has earned my place."

19. When you have the opportunity for the truth but choose to publish lies and the law holds you up for accountability, do not cry for mercy. Be bold as you were stupid in telling your lies and face the music of your folly.

20. What is more disorienting than a bad food? Is it more disorienting if you paid for it? It can throw your whole day into confusion.

21. The voice of fools and the voice of the wise are clear and distinct. "I want to be President". How reckless? How can you say that, when you have no vision to fix the economy, build roads and energy infrastructure or solve the food insecurity? The wise would sell his vision, the children of God would hear his voice; they could cry to the God of Heaven on his behalf and he shall be the leader of his people. The fool would buy the media, the people and the mercenaries and by spike God allows him. He would only end up with thorns and arrows at his side. And upon his children would untold curses remain eternal.

22. The wise only dreams of what his vision allows and not out of ego or ambition.

23. How foolish you are! You think this status quo would remain forever? The time would come, that time is already here, when all those who built their empire on this vanity would be put to shame.

24. Do not be deceived by those who claim to be equal to God or can make you so. Be humble, wise and observant. Be human before Him who gives life. Even the frog, if fed with fat, can it grow as big as the elephant? It is all deception. Meet God in your heart.

25. Knowing is everything to the child but to the wise, knowing is not enough. It is only part of knowing. Ananse puts it this way: "Knowing is only part of knowing."

26. You have to be blessed by God to fully enjoy the riches of this earth in Peace and Harmony.

27. Pray to Mother Earth that she would give you her milk. Protect her, care for her and treat her tenderly and she would give you her riches.

28. I hear you call yourself the President, Cabinet Minister, God-father, or a Kingmaker. When you reflect on the situation of your people, do you see yourself in a pool of looted resources or you see your people living happily because you have built hospitals, sustained industries or provided food and security?

29. Let the African youth who are fearful of the future, never lose heart. Dream again.

30. Listen and watch carefully. The world is not made up of only black and white colours. There are a million colours, much of which is not yet seen by the human eye.

31. Skin colour matters. Skin colour does not matter. Strange shifting viewpoints. Only two people would make an issue out of this. They are a child and a manipulator.

32. Ananse advises that, "If you have nothing to say, the best option to you is to keep your mouth shut and hold your tongue. Why open your mouth and say something stupid to embarrass yourself."

33. A good tea is medicinal to the body, soul and the whole being of a man. It does more good than the soothing rhetoric of politicians.

34. You want to see a miracle? Do not look far. Build a good road through a jungle and terminate it on a riverbank, spice it with a hospital and a basic school and watch what miracle it would bring forth.

35. Be careful when asked to go to battle. You may be the hand that destroys your own home. Fight the battles you know of.

36. Sometimes what is needed for your healing is to do nothing but to rest, kill sometime off, be with your family and friends.

37. Imagine. Imagination is the stairs to creativity and the birth of ingenuity.

38. Do you know that to be lucky you have to be prepared, anticipate and learn to acquire unique skills, lest luck would elude you?

39. Everybody pays a price. Every great man or successful person for that matter paid a price. That is the law of this planet called Earth whether you are a Christian, a Muslim, or a Buddhist. You must pay the price. The voice of God paves the way for the Earth to take note of you but to enjoy the oil of the earth, you must pay the price.

40. Of the entire price the great pay for their success, none tells of the actual price paid. They only infer it, confuse or blur it. Perhaps they are afraid of it or it was too high a price. Ananse says, "No one...no one talks of his real price." They only lament their troubles and failures. Did Ananse tell of the price for his wisdom?

41. Fools are dangerous and an uncontainable threat to any society, institutions and homes harbouring them. They must be searched, rounded up and hounded out. Do not suffer a fool for a second.

42. Does the hungry of the world need Genetically Modified (GM) foods? Our leaders say, "Of course we do". But our leaders do not eat GM foods. Ananse, help us. What do we do?

43. A time would come when your body would fail you and what you would desire would be your achievement. So if you are wise, follow Ananse's wisdom, "Get education; at all cost get skills. Without them, you would not be even proud of yourself."

44. Through creativity and hard work, you can overcome and achieve your dream.

45. Ironies of war;
   45.1. There are those who create wars.
   45.2. There are those who fight the wars.
   45.3. There are those who die in the wars.
   45.4. There are those who are blamed for the wars.
   45.5. There are those who make fortunes from the wars.
   45.6. There are those who come out as heroes.
   45.7. There are those who, out of the wars, discover themselves and go on to become pillars of society.
   45.8. There are those who lose everything in the wars.
   45.9. Every war creates its heroes and villains; losers and winners.

46. Sometimes, winning is not enough;
   46.1. Sometimes victory does not bring satisfaction.
   46.2. It neither guarantees rest nor peace of mind.
   46.3. Sometimes you would have to deal with your enemies in a manner that is ruthless, and merciless even though you would leave in your heart a stain, which no amount of water or prayers can wash away.
   46.4. Sometimes what has to be done would have to be done.
   46.5. Yes, noble men sometimes would have to do deeds, which are not noble.
   46.6. This is the world of men where Light is not the ruler. This too is part of God's world.
   46.7. Ananse says, "Understand this and you would preserve your life, fail to grasp and you would be blotted out."

47. A battle cry inspires champions and challenges the warrior; the same fills poets with anger; historians get itchy hands, and cowards die over and over again even as they hide in caves.

48. Man is a creed onto himself. If we shall hold the truth, our religion is one; "To love and to adhere to our divinity. Where we shall protect our bodies, each other and our society, and Mother Earth. All divine laws are blessed and handed by The MOTHER who conceives and gives birth to all."

49. War and Anarchy in the most glorious name;
49.1. Jesus came for Peace and in His name, He prayed for peace to dwell in the hearts of men but in His name peace has been butchered than in any other name in recorded history.
49.2. In his name more wars have been fought as many as in the name of Satan if not more;
49.3. In His name, more men and women have been killed than in any other name.
49.4. In His name, genocides have been committed, races have been exterminated and nations brought to ashes.
49.5. What can we say about this?
49.6. Ananse can only utter that, "The evil in the hearts of men blinded by ego, pride, domination and control has found a home in religion and Glorious Jesus slandered."
49.7. Jesus is still The LORD

50. Your nation falters because it was built on lies;
50.1. Your nation slumbers because it was built on personalities,
50.2. Your beloved nation is no longer loved because it was built on a cult.
50.3. O yes, the society you love no longer prospers because it was built on a false foundation,
50.4. A nation built on the foundation of truth, honesty, love, integrity, harmony and positive attitudes is the only true nation, which can last.
50.5. And if the sons and daughters shall uphold these values eternally, they would last a millennium.

51. Warriors, forever fighting, forever planning;
51.1. One battle ends and they move on to the other.
51.2. In this they find peace and fulfilment.
51.3. Who would tell them to stop?
51.4. Who can say, "It is over?"
51.5. Pitiful creatures with whose plight we the masses find peace.
51.6. At night they roll on their beds in pains and groans, restless of uncertainty
51.7. As they hope of the coming day.

51.8. O see their faces in the heat of war; they are so lovely, comforting and at peace.

51.9. From those faces, we the poor mortals know we are safe.

51.10. Safe from our enemies;

51.11. Safe from fear itself.

51.12. But they are never at peace; never at rest;

51.13. One battle ends, another starts.

52. What does the warrior do when the battles are over?

52.1. Does he put his house in order and depart this tent?

52.2. Does he play golf?

52.3. Does he write his memoirs?

52.4. Does he seek other wars and come to ruin?

52.5. Does he sleep all day?

52.6. How does he cure his restlessness?

52.7. How would he dissipate all the energies built?

52.8. Does he sleep his remaining days away?

52.9. Does he drink, eat and kill his body?

52.10. All who seek to rise must know before the first battles?

52.11. What does the Warrior do in peace times?

53. Of architects, builders and teachers; there is no end; there is rest; there is no farewell. It is always moving on; lasting battles they embrace and settle for.

54. When the mind receives and holds true, the work is done. All that is left thereafter is for the Elohim to Decree and Time would Deliver.

55. The birth of light;

55.1. I have been pregnant for the past seven years,

55.2. I have been in birth pains for the past 9 month,

55.3. The time of delivery is here with me,

55.4. Let all the worlds hear and sons of light rejoice,

55.5. The Light is born; beauty is born,

55.6. Let all the world groan in pain; their world is at an end,

55.7. This is a gift to the world. I am the light,

55.8. My Time is here,

55.9.   I give birth to the city of light, the city of gold.

56.   No man is in control. He can only slide it slightly. Power is in control. That is why one person leaves, another takes over and he still wields authority. Power never left because a poor mortal left a post. His throne is created and decrees established.

*In this affair of fire, tears and pain called life,*
*Only seven I ask for myself:*
*A place to lay my head;*
*That I will rise and not fall;*
*That I will know the peace of GOD all my life;*
*That my children shall follow my steps in the house of the LORD and be*
*provided for;*

"The achievements of the gods of our universe are regarded as
ground-breaking,
Unprecedented, revered and worshipped.
They transcend race, colour and profession.
They travel timelessly in time. They are rare.
Their abilities are beyond human imagination.
They are the gods among men or lived among men.
In life or death, they have the power to influence the affairs of men,
With words they long spoke, the silence of their absence or their names.
Their names have come to stand for certain good,
Values or a course able to direct and enhance human endeavours."

From: THE DREAMS OF OUR YOUTH
Ananse says, "This is my ultimate goal."

*And now, look at those you see on your electronic visual boxes*
*And hear of them as messiahs.*
*Are they not phony?*
*Are they not empty?*
*Do they not look miserable?*
*If you listen to them very often, prepare for anarchy.*
*If you believe them, prepare for anxiety and a painful death,*
*Because their tongues carry fires of hell and death.*
*Are they not prisoners themselves?*

*These are the solemn revelations of Ananse,*
*I am a form of David*
*I am a form of Moses*
*I am a form of Solomon*
*I am a combination of all*
*Living and reliving their brails*
*I would see my kingdom rise and not fall*
*I would live to an old age, behold the promised land*
*and live on it the rest of my life.*
*I would not die at the House of idols*
*I am the beloved of the LORD GOD ALMIGHTY*
*The ELOHIM holds me protected and accountable*

# Index

## A

Abilities 24, 58, 85, 151, 171, 184, 197, 199, 238
Absolution 20, 66
Abuja 50, 197
Abundance v, 29, 49, 55, 106, 112, 147, 171, 186, 199, 229
Abused 58, 198
Accountability 197, 200, 230
Accountable 109, 123, 162, 205, 240
Accra 197, 217
Achievable 12
Achieve 13, 14, 23, 40, 53, 63, 72, 74, 96, 107, 112, 176, 178, 186, 188, 192, 202, 207, 209, 214, 217, 220, 223, 225, 233
Achieved 14, 36, 58, 119, 143, 147, 201, 214, 223
Achievements 19, 52, 118, 119, 176, 214, 238
Act i, 24, 39, 75, 84, 97, 107, 109, 128, 143, 145, 156, 162, 177, 184
Action 13, 15, 39, 148, 162
Actions 65, 71, 86, 93, 103, 109, 119, 122, 123, 124, 132, 170, 225
Acts 37, 46, 80, 113, 133, 145
Adamu 43
Adapt 79, 86
Adaptations 45
Adulations 24, 42, 44, 58, 66, 89, 107, 140, 210, 216
Advantage 40
Adversity 31
Afraid 44, 66, 68, 73, 119, 177, 207, 232
Africa 21, 22, 26, 39, 40, 74, 88, 91, 106, 108, 118, 124, 125, 129, 184, 187, 192, 198, 200, 204, 224

African 25, 72, 87, 89, 90, 106, 107, 112, 124, 180, 224, 225, 231
African Elite 106, 107
Africans 39
Age 37, 59, 63, 66, 85, 88, 102, 107, 151, 160, 166, 171, 183, 215, 216, 240
Air vii, 22, 39, 40, 63, 127, 220, 229
Albert Einstein 71, 95, 220
Alien 61
Ally 45
Ambition 74, 106, 179, 215
America 181, 187, 188
Ananse 6, 13, 14, 15, 16, 17, 19, 20, 22, 24, 33, 36, 38, 39, 41, 44, 45, 47, 51, 52, 53, 55, 56, 57, 59, 62, 65, 66, 67, 68, 73, 89, 94, 96, 101, 102, 106, 107, 113, 119, 123, 128, 134, 135, 136, 141, 143, 144, 145, 151, 152, 158, 159, 162, 163, 164, 166, 167, 170, 171, 172, 177, 180, 183, 184, 186, 188, 189, 192, 193, 197, 198, 201, 202, 207, 209, 213, 214, 215, 216, 218, 220, 221, 222, 223, 224, 227, 231, 232, 233, 234, 238, 240
Ananse Verses 6, 57, 218
Anarchy ii, 9, 10, 32, 38, 63, 115, 222, 239
Angel 4, 87, 88
Anglican 31
Anguish 88
Animal 54, 55, 68, 95, 109, 166, 178, 189
Animals 54, 90, 102, 109, 139, 188, 223
Antha Diop 13, 192
Anxiety vii, 4, 38, 54, 71, 73, 79, 84, 87, 105, 113, 149, 239
Apathy 151
Appetites 63, 101, 164, 201
Architects 71, 135, 141, 235

Army 26, 63, 102, 184
Arrogance 24, 123, 181, 205
Arrows 230
Ascend 11, 18, 142, 218
Ascension 38, 199
Ascent vi, 92
Ashes 90, 221, 225, 234
Ask 14, 25, 27, 33, 37, 44, 52, 55, 58,
    65, 67, 85, 89, 101, 112, 126,
    132, 136, 166, 193, 202, 221,
    237
Aspirations 78, 84, 123
Assassinations 38
Attitude 194, 199
Attitudes 78, 81, 85, 107, 157, 167,
    180, 187, 202, 234
Authority 41, 44, 171, 236

**B**

Bad 22, 51, 67, 75, 77, 79, 148, 183,
    209, 230
Balance 25, 30, 52, 64, 68, 69, 72, 162,
    163, 171, 194, 202, 223
Bankrupt 68
Banquet v, 35
Bargain 95
Battle 6, 12, 22, 24, 25, 37, 115, 122,
    148, 173, 189, 207, 224, 228,
    232, 233, 234, 235
Battles 12, 18, 30, 33, 48, 67, 68, 72,
    122, 145, 225, 228, 232, 235
Bearer 89, 101
Bearer 89, 101
Beautiful 12, 21, 44, 45, 65, 67, 96,
    106, 118, 133, 145, 159, 171,
    188, 192, 194, 227, 229
Beautiful mind 12
Beauty 2, 11, 21, 37, 41, 42, 53, 54, 61,
    64, 71, 80, 85, 86, 90, 109, 114,
    145, 164, 179, 189, 229, 235
Beggars 199
Beginning 30, 50, 104, 112, 186

Beijing 181, 188
Believe 10, 25, 42, 78, 112, 115, 122,
    145, 156, 162, 165, 176, 178,
    185, 186, 193, 225, 229, 239
Believed 17, 19, 67, 116, 220
Believer 26
Believing 225
Bermuda 17
Best x, 30, 47, 50, 51, 54, 55, 68, 75,
    78, 81, 85, 93, 126, 141, 171,
    173, 181, 189, 198, 208, 213,
    218, 219, 220, 231
Betrayal 32, 33, 55, 80, 83
Beware 20, 123, 133, 151, 158, 162,
    209, 220
Biblical 83
Big 1, 41, 61, 113, 118, 123, 135, 140,
    141, 165, 175, 194, 197, 201,
    205, 230
Big dreamers 118
Billionaire ix, 174, 216
Birth v, 8, 41, 50, 65, 71, 109, 114,
    115, 136, 171, 173, 232, 233,
    236
Black 109, 123, 231
Blackmail 207
Blackmailed 77, 227
Blame 22, 93, 108, 132, 181, 188
Blessings 16, 36, 51, 100, 167, 214,
    216, 221
Blind 12, 63, 153, 165
Blinded 53, 134, 183, 234
Bliss 23, 47, 64, 65, 66, 115, 143, 199,
    200, 215
Blood viii, 7, 18, 45, 64, 73, 83, 101,
    114, 126, 129, 147, 153, 159,
    161, 167, 173, 200, 216
Bloodshed 38, 201
Body viii, 12, 14, 20, 29, 42, 46, 52,
    58, 59, 69, 72, 97, 101, 108,
    109, 113, 128, 129, 134, 140,
    141, 151, 155, 186, 194, 197,
    199, 214, 221, 231, 232, 235

Bold 54, 78, 124, 128, 134, 204, 230
bomb 61, 229
Bondage 31
Books 53, 66, 67, 136, 144, 171, 180,
    184, 192, 227
born 217
Boss 21
Box 95, 119, 208
Boys 16
Brain 7, 43
Brand 36, 187
Breast 125, 183
Brother viii, 79, 101, 109, 112, 131,
    139, 141, 161, 195
BSc 128
Build vi, vii, 32, 39, 40, 43, 44, 53,
    62, 65, 66, 77, 82, 96, 100, 107,
    113, 124, 127, 140, 160, 162,
    166, 177, 179, 187, 200, 221,
    226, 230
Builders 22, 235
Bunkers 11
Burden 23, 36, 66, 72, 73, 119, 168,
    176, 200
Burn viii, 138

**C**

Caged 163
Calamity 40, 141
Calf 197
Call 11, 24, 39, 42, 84, 88, 90, 95, 103,
    106, 112, 125, 139, 142, 149,
    158, 159, 183, 189, 209, 213,
    224, 231
Calm 84, 170
Campaign 65, 184
Carbon 204
Care 10, 13, 21, 32, 37, 51, 125, 172,
    204, 215, 231
Career 194, 198, 213
Careless 14
Carry 25, 51, 68, 91, 158, 189, 239

Cataclysm 40
Cautions 20
Caves 113, 233
Centuries ii
Certificate 13, 156, 178
Chains 10, 68, 80, 103, 124, 148, 194,
    227
Challenges 29, 39, 78, 79, 84, 100,
    107, 132, 158, 178, 198, 208,
    209, 233
Champions 53, 57, 143, 233
Change 25, 37, 40, 50, 65, 80, 84, 91,
    101, 112, 115, 122, 126, 156,
    157, 158, 167, 172, 173, 179,
    180, 181, 188, 192, 201
Chaos 44, 71, 96, 100, 115, 141, 194
Character 10, 56, 74, 87, 135, 157
Charity 170
Cheat 93, 156, 170
Cherish 90, 114, 227
Chess x, 219
Chief Executive 15
Child viii, 150
Children vii, 1, 2, 7, 12, 15, 16, 21,
    22, 23, 24, 29, 31, 36, 37, 40,
    42, 44, 50, 51, 54, 58, 62, 63,
    66, 73, 74, 78, 80, 85, 87, 88,
    89, 98, 100, 101, 103, 109, 113,
    114, 118, 121, 129, 139, 143,
    152, 153, 159, 183, 187, 192,
    198, 200, 210, 213, 216, 217,
    222, 223, 225, 230, 237
Chimpanzees 73
China 40, 187
Choice vii, 44, 51, 58, 59, 93, 98, 99,
    128, 135, 142, 181, 198, 210,
    211
Choices 79, 98, 100, 128, 129, 132,
    143, 167
Christ Jesus 56
Christos 84
Chronicles 19, 52
Church iii, 31, 65, 96, 97, 98, 207, 227

Cities 39, 57, 83

Citizens 72, 73, 77, 118, 221, 223

City 1, 159, 210, 236

Civilization 228

Class 45, 69, 93, 94, 128, 141, 192

Classes 167

Clock 84, 113

Code 119, 141, 224

Colleagues 80, 90

Colossus 24, 25, 185

Colours 93, 94, 116, 129, 231

Comfort 32, 33, 51, 55, 56, 77, 79, 91, 94, 119, 125, 132, 162, 171, 172, 178, 193, 202, 208, 210

Common interest 39, 93, 94

Common-sense 192

Compass 201

Compassion 93

Competitors 151

Conceive 112, 171, 201

Confess 59, 221

Confident 85, 128, 180

Confusion 175, 186, 230

Conquer 57, 63, 81, 96, 139, 151, 170, 184, 202, 216, 217

Conqueror 89, 118

Conquerors 53

Conscience 65, 85, 128, 164, 167, 200, 215, 220

Consciousness 47, 112, 129

Content 30, 77, 214

Contentment 11, 66, 72, 123, 136, 214

Continent 29, 43, 87, 112, 124, 129, 224

Control 11, 36, 42, 44, 46, 68, 71, 79, 115, 149, 157, 158, 194, 234, 236

Conviction 178, 185, 199, 228

Corporation 72

Corruption 163, 183, 184

Cost 51, 77, 87, 90, 177, 189, 193, 204, 232

Council vii, 87, 111

Counsel 100, 108, 124, 129, 179, 208, 223

Country 77, 221

Covenants 216

Cowardice 21, 128

Cowards 125, 173, 233

Crafty men 65

create ix, 10, 13, 16, 21, 53, 68, 69, 71, 72, 77, 78, 80, 108, 112, 113, 115, 136, 149, 151, 162, 167, 169, 173, 209, 213, 217, 233

Creating vi, 12, 82, 95, 115, 118, 147, 209, 210

Creation 16, 83, 114, 165, 200, 224, 229

Creativity 114, 232, 233

Creator 18, 187, 215

Creators 27, 83, 103, 119, 124, 210

Creature viii, 18, 93, 161, 170

Creed 52, 98, 128, 225, 233

Cries of the needy v, 8

Crime 53, 93, 141

Cronies 221

Cross 80, 214, 229

Crucify 53

Crusader 167

Cry v, vii, 8, 25, 37, 83, 89, 101, 108, 121, 153, 186, 214, 230, 233

Cultural 108, 129

Cultural agent 108

Cunning 73, 171, 179, 183, 207

Curiosity 11

Curse 23, 37, 45, 152, 165, 225

Curses 19, 157, 230

Cycle 27, 50, 64, 71, 84, 115, 135, 159, 160, 170, 205

**D**

Damned 72, 75

Dances 21, 27

Dangerous 44, 61, 97, 232

Dangote 72

Dare 26, 55

Dark 6, 20, 54, 74, 144, 228

Darkness 1, 11, 31, 59, 79, 89, 100, 134, 136, 137, 186, 199, 224

David 240

Day 1, 11, 12, 13, 14, 18, 23, 42, 43, 45, 52, 53, 56, 65, 75, 77, 83, 91, 97, 102, 106, 112, 123, 125, 135, 141, 142, 144, 158, 159, 163, 167, 186, 192, 194, 200, 202, 205, 209, 210, 213, 214, 217, 224, 227, 230, 234, 235

Daydreaming 209

Dead 44, 47, 53, 164, 173

Debt viii, 65, 109, 136, 161

Deception 178, 194, 198, 228, 230

Decision 18, 101, 132, 184, 188, 197, 202, 229

Decisions 41, 68, 79, 132, 171, 183, 193

Defeat 37, 67, 193

Demons 23, 134, 184

Deny 19, 38, 68, 120, 132, 201, 224

Descendants 19, 73, 87

Desire 40, 42, 73, 86, 118, 145, 158, 162, 188, 199, 232

Desolation 228

Destiny 17, 23, 79, 80, 124, 142, 157

Destroy 11, 19, 54, 58, 63, 69, 101, 120, 134, 160, 162, 178, 189, 214, 221

Destructive 17, 61

Determination 192, 213

Developed 61, 198

Development 85, 101, 156, 157, 162

Devil 31, 122, 149, 198, 201

Devotion 2, 12

Diet 59

Dig 223, 224

Dignity vi, 10, 14, 16, 26, 36, 40, 51, 75, 79, 81, 90, 92, 104, 119, 123, 143, 151, 170, 171, 176,

184, 209, 213, 214

Dimensions 32, 205

Discipline 42

Diseases 29, 53, 71, 88, 114, 128

Disgrace vi, 33, 92

Disobey 20

Diversities 107

Divine 18, 20, 32, 33, 44, 47, 52, 54, 59, 69, 95, 101, 109, 124, 129, 141, 143, 159, 168, 176, 194, 200, 210, 216, 227, 233

Divine plan 39

Divine use 20

Divorce 227

Doctors 166

Dogmas 194

Domination 11, 41, 45, 234

Donkey 158

Doors viii, 15, 22, 45, 93, 94, 102, 124, 146, 187, 215

Doubt ii, 62, 90, 128, 147, 181, 186

Downfall 65, 205

Dragon 24, 187

Dream iv, 12, 13, 14, 37, 40, 61, 79, 113, 114, 129, 151, 153, 157, 170, 173, 176, 178, 183, 187, 189, 192, 194, 199, 201, 202, 208, 215, 217, 225, 226, 233

Dreamer 224

Dreams 11, 12, 13, 15, 19, 39, 56, 61, 63, 72, 73, 74, 75, 77, 78, 79, 84, 85, 93, 95, 101, 118, 119, 122, 123, 128, 136, 151, 158, 165, 167, 168, 172, 177, 178, 183, 185, 186, 188, 189, 190, 192, 198, 201, 202, 207, 208, 209, 214, 215, 222, 223, 224, 225, 230

Drink v, 20, 47, 49, 50, 89, 159, 197, 213, 216, 221, 229

Drive 50, 113, 119, 133, 136, 151, 165, 167, 178, 198

Drug 97

Drunkard 61
Drunkards 95
Duty 37, 102, 108, 113, 148, 209, 210

# E

Eagles 24
Earn 73, 84, 168, 176, 181, 227
Earth ii, v, 18, 22, 25, 49, 50, 52, 53,
    62, 81, 89, 90, 102, 108, 118,
    200, 204, 216, 217, 231, 232,
    233
Easily 14, 106, 159, 177
Easy life 170
Eat vii, 20, 47, 80, 88, 112, 113, 127,
    133, 136, 159, 184, 193, 197,
    210, 213, 221, 227, 229, 232,
    235
Economic 26, 101, 166
Economists 68
Economy 230
Ecosystem 228
Educate iv, 43, 114, 163
Education 37, 38, 40, 44, 52, 79, 87,
    118, 178, 223, 232
Ego 24, 103, 124, 202, 230, 234
Elders 12, 39, 67, 78, 86, 220
Elite 106, 107
ELOHIM 16, 31, 61, 97, 98, 101, 109,
    113, 218, 235
Emerson 13
Emotions 62, 64, 100, 103, 140
Empires 77, 84, 113, 123, 217
Empowers 79, 230
Empty stomach 41, 225
Encyclopaedia 216
End vi, 12, 14, 18, 21, 22, 30, 36, 37,
    38, 43, 44, 46, 51, 52, 54, 79,
    83, 84, 87, 88, 92, 98, 102, 106,
    112, 120, 129, 135, 143, 144,
    151, 163, 164, 173, 184, 189,
    193, 194, 214, 216, 217, 218,
    229, 230, 235

Endeavours 65, 109, 194, 199, 238
Enemies 19, 26, 42, 87, 129, 141, 173,
    177, 180, 181, 193, 195, 214,
    223, 233, 235
Energies 14, 40, 46, 52, 80, 93, 107,
    120, 126, 156, 175, 235
Energy 39, 44, 45, 69, 73, 80, 108,
    112, 145, 188, 198, 204, 207,
    208, 225, 230
Engineers 54, 115
Enlightened 94, 106
Enthusiasm 107, 108, 199
Entrepreneurship 170
Environment 13, 31, 72, 78, 86, 119,
    120, 151, 156, 157, 167, 180,
    184, 192, 193, 210, 224
Envy 20
Eons 52, 123
Error x, 22, 202, 212
Escape 32, 59, 85, 164, 166
Eternal 18, 26, 30, 31, 43, 57, 77, 84,
    93, 104, 115, 133, 136, 223,
    227, 228, 230, 234
Eternal wars 31, 228
Eternity 19, 30, 31, 43, 47, 53, 66, 84,
    104, 106, 115, 132, 136, 223
Everest ix, 182
Evil ii, vi, viii, 11, 23, 37, 54, 61, 65,
    67, 70, 85, 87, 99, 102, 103,
    113, 115, 125, 131, 132, 143,
    145, 149, 163, 164, 176, 185,
    198, 200, 205, 210, 216, 222,
    225, 234
Evolution 39, 50
Exaggerate 193
Excellence 123
Excuses 84
Exist vi, 9, 10, 16, 17, 60, 64, 69, 71,
    87, 103, 115, 153
Expensive 213
Experience 148, 173, 180
Experiments 17, 83
Experts 80, 119

Exploiters 151

Eyes 12, 22, 26, 39, 44, 46, 63, 68, 74, 85, 90, 95, 109, 120, 159, 164, 166, 186, 192, 194, 213, 221, 231

# F

Facebook 148

Fail ii, 22, 44, 45, 62, 73, 77, 123, 142, 157, 185, 188, 200, 214, 215, 233

Failure 95, 97, 133, 166

Failures 61, 67, 80, 85, 158, 159, 172, 184, 204, 209, 213, 232

Faith vii, 43, 45, 112, 121, 187, 220

Fall vi, 17, 32, 65, 86, 90, 92, 128, 153, 164, 177, 185, 187, 189, 193, 200, 210, 220, 237, 240

False v, 8, 31, 39, 106, 113, 115, 133, 227, 234

Falsehood 1, 6

False religion 106

Fame 22, 53, 178, 215, 216, 220

Family v, 8, 10, 11, 15, 20, 26, 32, 86, 95, 109, 118, 139, 177, 202, 215, 216, 224, 225, 232

Famines 31

Fasting 55, 56, 97

Fatal 112, 180, 202

Fate 17, 19, 22, 68, 77, 95, 135, 214, 225

Father iii, viii, 18, 67, 71, 73, 112, 124, 161, 185, 194, 209

Father Markus 73

Fats viii, 62, 138, 223

Fatten 143, 197

Favour 11, 39, 101, 132, 133, 136, 168, 175

Fear 1, 4, 14, 20, 24, 32, 43, 84, 87, 90, 93, 101, 109, 113, 118, 128, 136, 175, 204, 235

Fed 38, 106, 112, 135, 143, 172, 216, 230

Fight 12, 14, 23, 26, 47, 54, 57, 67, 68, 72, 96, 98, 101, 115, 139, 141, 148, 151, 158, 171, 173, 185, 200, 209, 233

Fire 16, 33, 65, 91, 114, 153, 198, 200, 228, 237

Fires 11, 33, 57, 91, 147, 223, 239

Flee 197

Flesh v, 8, 11, 18, 26, 41, 44, 45, 46, 47, 52, 63, 64, 65, 77, 80, 86, 96, 97, 100, 113, 114, 124, 129, 136, 145, 152, 153, 159, 164, 183, 193, 194, 200, 215, 218, 221

Float 11, 172

Focus 27, 187, 198

Focused 63

Folly 21, 22, 58, 107, 118, 129, 159, 160, 179, 181, 198, 200, 230

Food ii, 1, 15, 19, 20, 25, 26, 29, 31, 37, 41, 44, 52, 55, 59, 61, 63, 66, 88, 96, 100, 109, 114, 125, 126, 132, 140, 148, 159, 172, 197, 207, 221, 225, 229, 230, 231

Fool 17, 23, 24, 36, 41, 51, 54, 58, 64, 65, 66, 79, 95, 100, 115, 124, 132, 144, 164, 166, 185, 192, 194, 200, 201, 220, 227, 230, 232

Fools 22, 23, 24, 27, 43, 44, 50, 58, 157, 186, 189, 190, 220, 230

Footprints 123, 201, 214

Footstool 189

Force 9, 37, 61, 64, 74, 122, 133, 140, 198

Forces 64, 71, 80, 159, 200

Foresight 21, 125, 178, 216

Forgiveness viii, 34, 131, 144

Fortresses 87, 91

Fortune ix, 32, 77, 157, 173, 182, 185, 199, 213

Forward 1, 39, 43, 52, 79, 86, 89, 107, 157, 163, 167, 180, 208

Foundation v, 28, 42, 163, 213, 234

Free 1, 31, 32, 47, 54, 57, 64, 66, 95, 97, 100, 101, 103, 104, 109, 115, 133, 135, 136, 171, 194, 210, 217, 218, 221, 230

Freedom vii, viii, 1, 4, 14, 29, 51, 54, 56, 57, 62, 64, 66, 68, 79, 93, 100, 101, 102, 105, 110, 120, 122, 133, 134, 161, 165, 172, 194, 198, 210, 211, 218, 222, 227, 230

Freethinking 51

Frequency 25

Friend 4, 85, 148, 157, 173, 181, 194, 204, 225

Fruit 223

Fulfilment v, 17, 25, 31, 36, 49, 56, 63, 96, 118, 157, 170, 176, 183, 201, 204, 208, 215, 217, 220, 234

Future vi, 21, 23, 39, 40, 42, 54, 82, 86, 107, 118, 123, 133, 134, 165, 205, 222, 223, 227, 231

**G**

Gain 27, 66, 107, 123, 159, 228

Galactic 148, 217

Game x, 95, 114, 115, 219

Gangsters 75

Gap 152, 180

Gatekeepers 88, 95

Gaze 22

Generation 39, 108, 118, 123, 158, 163, 176, 225

Generations 21, 123, 129, 143, 158, 176, 192

Generous iii, 108, 143, 185, 187

Genocide 83

Gift v, 18, 26, 28, 44, 47, 67, 126, 135, 179, 235

Global 224

Globalization 78

Glory vii, 18, 21, 24, 36, 50, 53, 54, 64, 86, 105, 122, 129, 142, 152, 177, 188, 229

Glow 21, 114, 179

Glutton 140

Goals viii, 14, 67, 78, 107, 115, 125, 138, 150, 177, 178, 179, 180, 183, 199, 208, 223

God iii, vii, viii, 1, 2, 26, 34, 37, 45, 56, 57, 71, 80, 84, 87, 88, 89, 90, 93, 100, 103, 105, 112, 114, 124, 136, 143, 144, 145, 149, 161, 178, 188, 229, 237, 240

Godfather 231

Gods v, 8, 11, 17, 22, 42, 55, 63, 66, 77, 95, 98, 104, 124, 217, 238

Gold 22, 32, 57, 58, 62, 64, 84, 104, 165, 193, 204, 210, 222, 227, 236

Golden 21, 65, 112

Good ii, vi, viii, ix, 11, 16, 18, 21, 22, 23, 27, 32, 33, 51, 52, 53, 55, 57, 58, 65, 66, 67, 70, 72, 74, 77, 85, 87, 96, 99, 101, 108, 113, 115, 116, 119, 125, 126, 128, 132, 143, 148, 151, 155, 162, 163, 164, 171, 172, 173, 176, 178, 179, 185, 186, 187, 190, 191, 193, 194, 200, 204, 213, 214, 216, 220, 221, 231, 238

Good counsel 179

Good counsel 179

Good man 22

Government vi, 70, 71, 72, 75, 113, 166, 180, 220, 221

Grace 11, 18, 22, 25, 29, 34, 36, 37, 43, 51, 58, 59, 89, 102, 136, 143, 159, 168, 185, 189, 221

Grandiose 14

Grateful iii, 47, 227, 229

Great  13, 14, 16, 21, 22, 31, 33, 39, 40, 43, 45, 47, 65, 69, 91, 109, 118, 119, 124, 125, 128, 143, 162, 163, 165, 172, 178, 186, 193, 200, 208, 216, 228, 229, 232

Greatest  38, 43, 55, 58, 62, 106, 148, 164, 177, 179, 185, 216

Great men  13, 172, 178

Greatness  ix, 29, 40, 118, 145, 168, 169, 170, 185, 199, 200, 217

Greed  18, 20, 36, 102, 107, 113, 123, 183

Greedy  36, 112, 122, 125, 139

Grow  1, 10, 14, 15, 18, 21, 42, 54, 62, 86, 96, 115, 126, 158, 183, 194, 199, 202, 205, 223, 230

Growth  10, 14, 29, 39, 56, 62, 84, 91, 108, 120, 123, 129, 134, 140, 180, 216

Grumble  72, 214

Guard  199

Guardian  62

Guardians  vii, 26, 127

Guerrilla  30

Guidance  iii, 128, 162, 192, 208, 223

Guns  44, 83

## H

Habits  157

Hallelujah  58

Happiness  1, 23, 38, 56, 67, 85, 88, 94, 136, 144, 157, 192, 199, 208, 214, 215, 227, 228

Happy  10, 13, 24, 31, 45, 56, 86, 93, 112, 115, 118, 149, 163, 185, 192, 195, 204

Hardworking  186

Harmony  ii, iv, 56, 71, 94, 109, 115, 134, 136, 141, 199, 215, 217, 229, 234

Hate  18, 20, 74, 93, 95, 177

Hatred  viii, 79, 113, 161

Haunted  23, 24, 68, 129, 170

Head  12, 14, 21, 118, 123, 124, 165, 170, 177, 213, 237

Headache  214

Healing  17, 45, 46, 58, 71, 97, 102, 122, 123, 125, 139, 141, 145, 164, 173, 221, 232

Health  12, 21, 29, 44, 56, 69, 94, 126, 134, 148, 214, 229

Health inspector  148

Healthy  20, 56, 59

Hear  v, x, 6, 8, 29, 43, 52, 58, 67, 77, 85, 93, 103, 113, 159, 165, 166, 176, 183, 213, 219, 230, 231, 235, 239

Hearts  iv, 22, 31, 94, 114, 116, 129, 136, 147, 193, 234

Heat  64, 148, 235

Heaven  ii, 26, 50, 53, 56, 71, 103, 109, 227, 230

Heavens  2, 11, 18, 71, 89, 129

Heights  vi, viii, 39, 68, 92, 95, 114, 122, 150, 218

Heiress  188

Hell  12, 53, 54, 142, 170, 215, 239

Hero  19, 74, 120

Heroes  16, 31, 51, 52, 74, 95, 120, 178, 233

Hide  1, 65, 132, 213, 233

Himalayas  187

Historians  233

History  210

Hole  197

Holiness  17, 18, 31, 51, 54, 84, 98, 134

Hollywood  83

Holy  14, 18, 51, 54, 55, 71, 74, 78, 97, 104, 125, 133, 202, 227

Holy Spirit  20

Home  v, 18, 19, 21, 35, 46, 50, 54, 67, 96, 132, 133, 134, 137, 141, 142, 156, 162, 167, 183, 188, 192, 194, 200, 201, 207, 224, 232, 234

Honest 30, 108, 158, 193

Honesty vii, 10, 30, 93, 101, 111, 123, 234

Honour 16, 36, 38, 44, 52, 54, 74, 90, 93, 94, 98, 104, 107, 110, 119, 123, 125, 133, 141, 142, 143, 151, 152, 157, 159, 189, 194, 204, 210, 213

Hope vii, ix, 23, 30, 57, 63, 74, 100, 107, 111, 120, 122, 143, 154, 157, 174, 177, 178, 186, 194, 200, 204, 221, 223, 225, 234

Hopelessness 77, 151, 180

Horizon 40, 52, 107, 159, 173, 188, 198, 208, 225

Hospitals 15, 91, 221, 231

Hour ix, 16, 27, 38, 40, 45, 47, 73, 75, 89, 112, 113, 129, 132, 142, 174, 198, 213, 223, 228

Human v, vi, 8, 10, 11, 17, 31, 39, 42, 45, 50, 58, 62, 68, 69, 76, 90, 95, 97, 100, 106, 112, 122, 128, 130, 132, 133, 134, 140, 158, 178, 183, 186, 193, 205, 208, 218, 230, 238

Humanity 14, 15, 37, 67, 74, 87, 88, 93, 109, 114, 123, 128, 133, 134, 141, 142, 149, 152, 163, 201, 207, 224, 229

Humiliation 33, 153

Humility 11, 38, 57, 58, 66, 101, 107, 136, 215

Hunger vii, 33, 38, 44, 54, 55, 58, 59, 80, 90, 105, 144, 158, 172, 201, 217, 228

Hungry 55, 67, 90, 140, 163, 232

Hunted down 26

Hunter 222

Hunting 93

Hurt 58, 90, 132, 204

Husband 86, 101, 202

Husbands 50, 51

Hygiene 128

**I**

I AM ix, 11, 12, 17, 24, 25, 26, 33, 38, 39, 43, 47, 51, 55, 66, 68, 86, 89, 100, 104, 115, 118, 123, 124, 135, 139, 140, 141, 142, 166, 170, 185, 188, 189, 191, 192, 199, 207, 208, 210, 215, 216, 220, 221, 229, 230, 235, 240

Icons 217

Ideals 140, 201

Ideas 65, 122, 147, 176, 209

Ignorance 129, 147, 171

Illusion 25, 204, 223

Imagination 77, 179

Imagine 31, 65, 232

Immortal 129, 140

Impatience 20

Impossible vi, 45, 54, 66, 76, 95, 112, 126, 159, 171, 176, 192, 201

Impurity 210

Infiniteness 112

Influence 71, 78, 87, 158, 220, 238

Infrastructures 226

Inner kingdom 83

Innocence 51, 65, 67, 143

Innovation 79, 101, 112, 118

Inspiration 41, 63, 79, 210, 228

Inspired 14, 143, 217

Inspiring 102

Intellect 30, 37, 112

Intelligent man 15

Inventors 22

Invincible 22, 31, 59

Invisible viii, 80, 146, 147, 200, 209

Ironies of war 233

# J

Jail 12
Jesters 141, 156
Judges 42
Journey ii, v, vi, vii, 16, 17, 18, 19, 27,
        38, 43, 49, 56, 65, 74, 79, 83,
        84, 86, 98, 99, 100, 101, 106,
        107, 113, 124, 126, 135, 136,
        139, 143, 153, 156, 159, 162,
        179, 188, 189, 214, 222, 223
Joy 13, 14, 31, 37, 38, 85, 134, 189,
        192, 210, 220, 228
Judge 20, 42, 74, 87, 88, 103, 141, 178,
        210, 215, 220
Judgment 59
Jump 22, 120, 205
Jungle 22, 120, 205
Justice 9, 10, 159

# K

Kaka 29
Keep 13, 14, 36, 52, 53, 63, 68, 72, 74,
        84, 95, 123, 126, 133, 144, 151,
        170, 179, 181, 194, 205, 209,
        231
Keepers 216
Keep growing 13
Key iii, 29, 38, 39, 58, 68, 75, 85, 100,
        103, 106, 135, 140, 159, 220
Khartoum 197
Kigali 197
Kill 1, 19, 65, 86, 109, 120, 124, 160,
        232
Killed 77, 83, 234
Kindness 139
King 41, 71, 116, 175
Kingdom 66, 83, 194, 221, 240
Kingmaker 231
Kings 58, 83, 132, 156, 159, 163, 199
Know ix, 6, 7, 14, 15, 22, 25, 29, 30,

31, 32, 33, 34, 36, 37, 39, 40,
42, 43, 44, 46, 47, 48, 50, 52,
53, 54, 57, 58, 59, 61, 62, 63,
64, 65, 66, 67, 68, 72, 73, 80,
83, 85, 87, 88, 89, 93, 97, 98,
100, 101, 106, 109, 112, 113,
115, 124, 129, 132, 135, 136,
139, 140, 141, 145, 156, 157,
158, 162, 165, 166, 167, 171,
177, 178, 179, 180, 181, 183,
185, 188, 189, 191, 193, 200,
204, 207, 208, 210, 214, 215,
217, 218, 220, 222, 223, 225,
228, 229, 232, 235, 237
Knowing 10, 25, 38, 46, 51, 67, 68,
        101, 142, 143, 153, 207, 228,
        231
Knowledge 21, 31, 37, 39, 42, 43, 45,
        53, 54, 57, 63, 66, 67, 73, 84,
        89, 95, 106, 107, 123, 134, 136,
        137, 166, 176, 180, 185, 195,
        209, 216, 218, 222
Kofi Annan 37, 207

# L

Ladder 58, 172, 189
Lagos 217
Lamb 102
Lamentations 33
Last war 22
Latent 147
Laugh 21, 47, 67, 125, 136, 141, 175,
        184, 193
Law 32, 116, 141, 210, 230, 232
Laws viii, 9, 15, 32, 44, 52, 57, 62, 71,
        89, 131, 136, 141, 215, 222,
        228, 233
Lawyers 166
Lead 9, 37, 40, 43, 45, 46, 65, 153,
        184, 205
Leader ix, 31, 85, 140, 147, 172, 185,
        191, 224, 225, 230

Leadership 119, 123, 163, 176, 200

Learn 15, 29, 30, 41, 42, 43, 45, 47, 53, 54, 57, 58, 65, 66, 78, 80, 85, 108, 123, 135, 136, 139, 143, 156, 163, 166, 175, 181, 184, 188, 192, 199, 207, 209, 232

Learner 45, 66, 156, 181

Learning 38, 43, 67, 85, 86, 87, 114, 129, 162, 164, 165, 166, 180, 181, 188, 209

Legend 19

Lessons 14, 42, 62, 73, 86, 119, 178, 189

Liberation 118, 148, 222, 229

Liberties 45, 93

Liberty 51, 210

Lie 24, 67, 71, 83, 94, 120, 123, 148, 162, 165, 176

Lies 9, 25, 29, 51, 53, 57, 62, 67, 91, 98, 113, 115, 136, 141, 158, 162, 179, 185, 192, 193, 194, 204, 208, 229, 230, 234

Life v, vi, ix, 2, 9, 11, 14, 16, 17, 21, 22, 26, 27, 28, 30, 32, 33, 34, 36, 38, 39, 42, 43, 46, 47, 49, 51, 53, 54, 55, 56, 63, 66, 67, 68, 69, 71, 74, 78, 79, 84, 85, 86, 90, 91, 94, 95, 96, 99, 100, 106, 108, 109, 113, 114, 118, 120, 125, 126, 128, 129, 136, 140, 143, 147, 156, 157, 159, 162, 163, 167, 170, 171, 172, 175, 178, 179, 180, 183, 185, 186, 187, 188, 189, 191, 192, 194, 195, 199, 201, 202, 204, 207, 208, 214, 215, 216, 221, 229, 230, 233, 237, 238, 240

Lifelong 66, 95, 120, 151, 159, 178, 189, 197

Light iv, 1, 14, 17, 18, 22, 23, 26, 31, 41, 42, 73, 79, 88, 89, 98, 100, 114, 133, 134, 136, 142, 154, 163, 172, 173, 179, 201, 204, 216, 228, 229, 235, 236

Light of God 32, 133

Limit 1, 36, 58, 147, 159, 177, 208

Lines viii, 15, 17, 22, 48, 74, 104, 106, 107, 146

Listen 68, 85, 88, 184, 220, 227, 229, 239

Little men 6, 20, 59, 139, 178

Live viii, ix, 1, 14, 18, 22, 23, 29, 30, 46, 47, 50, 51, 52, 53, 54, 63, 77, 78, 83, 84, 95, 96, 98, 104, 113, 115, 116, 119, 123, 125, 131, 133, 136, 145, 149, 152, 157, 165, 170, 171, 172, 173, 181, 196, 202, 210, 215, 217, 240

Lofty 1, 186, 201

Loneliness 114, 186

Look v, 8, 12, 14, 32, 42, 44, 102, 172, 184, 197, 216

Looters 18, 75

LORD 37, 55, 72, 90, 125, 153, 179

Lords 6, 17, 30, 44, 53, 61

Lose 11, 14, 36, 40, 42, 52, 56, 66, 68, 98, 119, 122, 123, 159, 164, 186, 187, 198, 221, 227, 231, 233

Love iv, vii, viii, 10, 14, 15, 18, 21, 30, 33, 37, 38, 41, 45, 47, 51, 53, 61, 62, 66, 71, 86, 87, 90, 93, 94, 97, 101, 108, 109, 111, 112, 113, 125, 126, 128, 129, 131, 136, 143, 144, 145, 158, 162, 175, 177, 185, 194, 202, 204, 220, 222, 226, 227, 229, 233, 234

Lover 89

Loyalty 32, 172, 175, 177

Luck 17, 33, 167, 175, 188, 232

Lucky 202, 232

Lusts 198

# M

Machines 83, 133
Mad 53, 71, 73
Madman 164, 201, 216
Madness 11, 15, 17, 73, 91, 97, 159,
    160, 179, 207, 217
Man iv, x, 4, 10, 15, 17, 18, 19, 22, 25,
    29, 31, 32, 33, 36, 41, 42, 43,
    44, 51, 54, 57, 58, 61, 63, 66,
    67, 79, 81, 83, 84, 85, 86, 90,
    93, 94, 95, 101, 102, 104, 106,
    107, 109, 110, 112, 113, 115,
    120, 124, 128, 130, 132, 133,
    136, 140, 143, 144, 145, 147,
    152, 154, 156, 158, 159, 163,
    168, 170, 175, 179, 180, 188,
    192, 194, 200, 202, 204, 209,
    210, 212, 213, 215, 216, 221,
    222, 223, 225, 227, 228, 231,
    232, 236
Manhood 46, 186
Manipulate 23, 62, 220
Manipulator 94, 231
Mankind 177
Marble 193
March 21, 73
Marketing 108
Marriage 93, 94, 126, 177, 227
Marry 93, 188, 227
Marrying 94
Masses vi, x, 44, 53, 59, 64, 70, 74, 95,
    108, 112, 115, 132, 135, 143,
    171, 172, 177, 179, 197, 201,
    207, 210, 212, 228, 234
Master 41, 43, 47, 67, 135, 140, 152,
    156, 172, 197, 211, 228, 229
Masters 63, 136, 199, 210
Material 15, 20, 21, 30, 52, 62, 72, 86,
    88, 91, 104, 108, 109, 112, 114,
    145, 153, 183, 197, 200, 216,
    228
Materialism 61, 226

Maturity 13, 31, 32, 37, 81, 124, 129,
    156, 165
Media 113, 141, 230
Medical Doctors 166
Medication 59, 125
Mediocrity 123
Men ii, iv, vi, vii, viii, 1, 6, 9, 13, 17,
    20, 30, 31, 45, 54, 58, 59, 61,
    65, 66, 68, 70, 71, 73, 74, 77,
    78, 80, 81, 84, 88, 89, 92, 93,
    94, 97, 100, 102, 105, 106, 113,
    122, 124, 131, 139, 143, 147,
    162, 165, 166, 172, 175, 176,
    178, 179, 185, 198, 201, 202,
    210, 213, 215, 216, 220, 227,
    233, 234, 238
Men of honour 74, 143, 210
Mental 119
Mental power 119
Mercenaries 230
Merciless 113, 118, 158, 233
Mercy 10, 112, 159
mess 20, 21, 222
Message 2, 9, 56, 57, 88, 102, 106,
    142, 167, 177, 228
Messenger v, 32, 35, 175
Messengers 104, 122, 217
Messiah 102
Messiahs 102
Meteors 88
Methodists 31
Methods 30, 210
Mighty 11
Millionaire 216
Mind 12, 20, 25, 29, 42, 45, 46, 47, 52,
    67, 78, 94, 100, 128, 129, 140,
    145, 151, 156, 159, 164, 185,
    194, 199, 201, 204, 205, 208,
    217, 230, 233, 235
Minerals 102, 188, 222
Minister 175, 231
Miracles 29, 204
Mirages 199

Misfortune 103, 173, 175, 193

Mistake 43, 58, 175, 202

Moment 26, 40, 46, 47, 64, 75, 96, 100, 125, 152, 171, 177, 197, 217

Moments iii, 16, 19, 46, 55, 59, 64, 66, 77, 79, 123, 149, 185, 186, 187, 228, 229

Money 36, 53, 55, 56, 108, 114, 143, 178, 215, 216

Monster 68, 71, 113

Moral 80, 141, 202, 228

Mortal 6, 17, 18, 24, 42, 55, 123, 143, 157, 202, 221, 223, 236

Mortality 32, 84, 107, 140, 223

Mortals ii, 1, 9, 13, 16, 17, 22, 24, 30, 42, 52, 63, 87, 142, 143, 157, 170, 227, 235

Moses 240

MOST HIGH vii, viii, 1, 2, 16, 19, 24, 37, 71, 105, 124, 136, 142, 148, 161, 183, 229

Mother v, 8, 11, 18, 21, 22, 25, 26, 27, 45, 49, 50, 58, 72, 81, 89, 90, 102, 106, 108, 118, 129, 153, 192, 194, 198, 200, 204, 216, 217, 231, 233

Mother Africa 21, 22, 26, 106, 108, 118, 129, 192, 198, 200, 204

Mother Earth v, 18, 22, 25, 49, 81, 89, 90, 102, 108, 118, 194, 216, 217, 231, 233

Mother Ghana 118

Mothers 21, 88, 114

Motion 180

Motivation 13, 79, 165, 193, 198

Mountain 1, 97, 100, 118, 170, 193

Move ii, x, 73, 79, 84, 86, 107, 116, 157, 163, 176, 187, 192, 193, 209, 219, 234

Mr President 197

Mud 24, 32, 189, 222

Murder 38, 71

Music 97, 140

Muslims 31

Mysteries 217

**N**

Naked 88, 90, 163

narrow path 32

Nation 23, 29, 58, 72, 73, 74, 75, 80, 86, 87, 95, 107, 108, 109, 113, 118, 119, 124, 129, 133, 147, 164, 183, 186, 198, 213, 216, 217, 221, 223, 234

Nations 25, 31, 39, 58, 77, 88, 118, 123, 139, 167, 200, 234

Needs v, 8, 9, 32, 37, 56, 107, 128, 154, 178, 214, 232

Neighbour 136, 222

New 39, 55, 107, 114, 115, 122, 125, 142, 147, 153, 158, 163, 164, 166, 167, 176, 179, 180, 209, 217

New world 153, 217

Nightmares 73, 83, 113

Noble ix, 12, 21, 32, 62, 68, 83, 84, 89, 107, 147, 174, 233

Noblemen 215

Noble mother 21

Nuggets 32, 62, 84, 119, 227

**O**

Observe 166, 220

Obsession 12

Old 11, 54, 89, 102, 107, 147, 148, 160, 164, 166, 171, 176, 209, 215, 216, 240

Opinions 79, 119, 167

Opportunities 36, 78, 79, 86, 94, 106, 147, 151, 152, 158, 163, 166, 167, 170, 179, 180, 187, 193, 208, 214

Opportunity 45, 65, 73, 94, 102, 110, 208, 230
Oppressed 12
Optimist 199
Oracle 54
Order 39
Orientation 167, 172, 180
Overcome vii, 11, 16, 18, 19, 32, 39, 45, 51, 53, 58, 63, 99, 105, 107, 118, 140, 214, 221, 233

## P

Pain vi, 32, 33, 37, 38, 40, 47, 51, 55, 59, 60, 62, 71, 73, 75, 79, 80, 84, 88, 101, 114, 136, 143, 148, 158, 164, 173, 176, 177, 185, 189, 192, 199, 208, 209, 210, 217, 227, 228, 235, 237
Palaces 50, 163, 201, 204
Parents 40, 85
Parrots 24, 213
Passion 15, 52, 97
Passions 14, 19, 98
Past iv, 23, 31, 61, 62, 227, 235
Pastors iii, 88
Path x, 11, 18, 21, 29, 30, 31, 32, 36, 38, 41, 46, 56, 57, 62, 67, 98, 101, 102, 112, 125, 129, 135, 136, 141, 151, 170, 180, 187, 206, 209, 210, 213, 215, 216, 221, 228
Patience 37, 81, 197, 217
Patient 39, 62
Pause 39, 89, 103, 184
Pay 16, 33, 37, 40, 51, 61, 66, 73, 120, 125, 142, 143, 165, 172, 176, 210, 220, 222, 232
P-Bomb 30
Peace ii, v, vii, 12, 14, 16, 23, 26, 28, 29, 31, 32, 36, 41, 45, 47, 52, 53, 67, 71, 85, 88, 93, 94, 105, 108, 109, 114, 115, 120, 128,

136, 141, 143, 152, 171, 175, 176, 194, 199, 202, 225, 228, 233, 234, 235, 237
Pen 75, 148, 189
Perception 11
Perdition 216
Perfect 11, 43, 123, 187, 199
Peril 162, 192
Periods 186, 187
Perseverance 61, 79, 180, 199, 202, 217
Persons 17, 85, 122, 172, 178
Perspective 57, 156, 172, 179
Pestilence 88
Pet 168, 172, 179
Physics 220
Picture 140, 141, 193
Pigs 57, 73, 164
Pillar 25
Pillars 63, 221, 233
Pity ix, 19, 55, 136, 170, 188, 203
Plague 87, 88
Plan 30, 38, 213
Planet 40, 52, 62, 106, 109, 112, 141, 170, 200, 202, 232
Planning 84, 119
Plants 139, 188
Poets 233
Poise 21, 25, 115, 118
Poison 20, 59, 62, 69, 106, 114, 140, 145, 156, 159, 214, 221
Politician 15, 55, 148, 207, 225
Politics 165, 207
Poor 13, 17, 19, 42, 52, 53, 55, 56, 73, 90, 100, 108, 112, 157, 164, 167, 170, 176, 187, 192, 202, 222, 235, 236
Positive 61, 62, 77, 234
Potent 17, 30, 139, 144, 145, 179
Potentials 13, 62, 156, 198
Poverty viii, 39, 40, 101, 144, 146, 167, 187, 210, 217, 222
Power ii, 1, 7, 11, 17, 18, 25, 30, 31,

37, 40, 41, 51, 57, 59, 61, 62,
71, 72, 75, 80, 102, 103, 112,
113, 114, 116, 119, 122, 135,
136, 159, 171, 179, 202, 215,
224, 238
Powerful 7, 10, 12, 58, 69, 71, 77, 80,
110, 122, 133, 136, 164
Power of God 25, 112
Praised 85
Pray 21, 25, 30, 37, 42, 58, 59, 62, 129,
141, 142, 200, 223, 229
Prayer 87, 153, 221
Preferential 72
Pregnancy 227
Prepare 21, 40, 44, 46, 55, 156, 172,
185, 222, 239
Prepares 15, 73, 194
Present iv, ix, 42, 79, 106, 115, 118,
169, 227
President 39, 166, 177, 197, 230, 231
Pretences vi, 99, 172
Price 13, 15, 16, 19, 20, 33, 37, 39, 40,
43, 45, 51, 54, 61, 66, 84, 87,
113, 119, 125, 132, 136, 142,
143, 153, 165, 171, 172, 176,
192, 210, 217, 220, 222, 229,
232
Priceless 205
Pride 20, 26, 40, 118, 143, 157, 160,
170, 175, 217, 234
Princesses 129, 204
Principles 17, 140
Priorities 123, 208
Private 12, 166, 175, 181
Problem 16, 29, 39, 132, 152
Problems 29, 39, 53, 59, 132
Procedure 12, 119, 176
Process 30, 32, 46, 67, 68, 95, 108,
159, 210
Professionals 112, 163, 164, 225
Profit 73
Profitable 94
Progressive ideas 65

Promise vii, 14, 26, 44, 55, 77, 105,
158, 240
Promise land 240
Promises 123
Prophet 216
Prophets 31, 96
Prosper 61, 77, 91, 132, 152, 156
Prosperity 26, 57, 68, 73, 133, 180,
194, 216, 228
Protect vii, 9, 23, 37, 51, 54, 62, 65,
72, 102, 104, 126, 127, 128,
144, 198, 200, 210, 217, 233
Protection 9, 15, 26, 44, 51, 102, 125,
181
Protector 89, 90, 113, 143, 164, 181
Protects 9, 22, 67, 118, 163, 183
Proud 14, 19, 51, 108, 115, 165, 193,
213, 232
Provider 86
Public 12, 13, 19, 51, 52, 73, 97, 108,
181, 207, 221
Puppet 119, 162
Puppets 73, 181, 220
Purity 2, 15, 17, 122, 134
Purpose 23, 26, 27, 34, 57, 95, 113,
119, 142, 145, 148, 173, 178,
189, 199, 200, 204, 229
Purse 73
Push 1

**Q**

Qualified 33
Question ii, 55, 71, 79, 136, 185, 186
Questions 33, 37, 85, 185, 207
Quit 148, 158
Quotations 166
**R**
Race 163, 184, 224, 238
Ramires 29
Rare iv, 44, 175, 180, 197, 199, 214,
238

Reach out 18, 42
Read 11, 53, 128, 144, 145, 171, 185, 218
Real 12, 17, 20, 32, 58, 66, 67, 83, 91, 136, 144, 147, 166, 180, 184, 194, 197, 202, 232
Reality 14, 19, 20, 25, 43, 63, 79, 140, 151, 152, 157, 170, 180, 183, 184, 194, 200, 201, 204, 215, 223
Reap viii, 131
Reason 13, 57, 69, 103
Rebellion 93
Rebirth 39, 91, 101, 216
Receive 1, 9, 18, 37, 81, 106, 118, 141, 204
Reckless 16, 62, 63, 64, 230
Redeem 199
Reform 147
Refuges 6, 141
Regime 91, 125
Religion viii, 11, 25, 31, 51, 57, 65, 66, 106, 133, 149, 161, 216, 233, 234
Remember 13, 14, 29, 36, 37, 42, 56, 64, 67, 73, 77, 88, 89, 103, 112, 123, 125, 139, 156, 162, 168, 171, 185, 195, 207, 208, 223, 228
Resist 214
Resources 15, 40, 61, 72, 73, 79, 106, 110, 112, 119, 156, 158, 180, 181, 184, 199, 207, 209, 222, 231
Respect 25, 108, 119, 172, 176, 181, 184, 223
Rest v, 12, 13, 14, 23, 26, 31, 43, 46, 47, 49, 53, 73, 74, 112, 129, 132, 136, 143, 171, 176, 197, 214, 228, 230, 232, 233, 235, 240
Restaurant 149
Revelations of Ananse 240

Reverence 21, 112
Revolution 37
Reward 23, 31, 37, 38, 53, 95, 118, 142, 175, 208
Rewards v, 35, 157, 170, 171, 184
Rhetoric 147, 207, 231
Rich 55, 72
Riches ix, 56, 72, 73, 174, 186, 231
Riddle 68
Righteous v, 1, 14, 18, 49, 103, 122, 125, 133, 167
Rights i, viii, 68, 150, 210
Rise ii, iv, 1, 2, 10, 15, 17, 18, 23, 31, 32, 39, 44, 55, 73, 91, 95, 104, 122, 123, 124, 136, 142, 147, 158, 168, 170, 175, 178, 186, 187, 201, 216, 235, 237, 240
Riskiest 94
Risks 135, 193, 207
Rivers vii, 40, 127, 136, 153
Robbed 77
Role 73, 106, 229
Roman Catholic Church 31, 65
Romantic 139, 215
Root 224
Rotten 11, 164
Route 13, 57, 61, 94, 172, 176, 201, 213
Rules 17, 32, 33, 136, 208
Run 11, 17, 26, 29, 45, 58, 90, 93, 109, 132, 134, 173, 188, 197, 200, 225
Runners 10, 132
Rush 36, 37, 46, 180
Ruthless 122, 123, 135, 233

**S**

Saboteurs 224
Sacrifices 13, 114, 143, 222, 223, 230
Safe 30, 32, 36, 39, 53, 61, 133, 197, 209, 235
Sages 22, 145, 176

Saints 31, 53, 78, 133, 134, 162

Salvation viii, 11, 29, 51, 54, 57, 59, 62, 100, 101, 102, 120, 143, 161, 193, 221

Satisfaction 13, 14, 22, 25, 208, 233

Save 40, 55, 75, 80, 89, 157, 164, 185, 202, 208

Saviour 59, 114, 153, 193

Scarcity 199

Sceptre of God 227

Schools 15, 44, 91

Scripted 44, 170

Sea 62, 175

Season 57, 162

Seat 19, 123, 139, 159, 166, 197, 213

Security 91, 115, 130, 132, 133, 148, 180, 197, 210, 228, 231

Seek 1, 10, 11, 12, 13, 20, 25, 40, 66, 68, 72, 84, 90, 93, 106, 122, 126, 129, 134, 147, 170, 177, 178, 210, 211, 217, 220, 224, 235

Seeker 1

Self 40, 47, 56, 78, 90, 109, 119, 124, 125, 143, 147, 152, 164, 167, 170, 179, 215

Self-criticism 125

Self-respect 119

Self-serving 147

Sensing 101

Servants 7, 176, 187

Serve 2, 9, 14, 119, 125, 140, 172, 201

Sex 41, 45, 52, 81, 96, 97, 133

Shadows 29, 32, 140, 216, 224

Shame 21, 153, 165, 197, 230

Share 15, 16, 78, 81, 134, 142, 165, 178, 181, 222

Shareholders 15, 72

She 21, 22, 23, 38, 46, 58, 67, 118, 129, 139, 152, 158, 164, 173, 181, 189, 198, 200, 216, 227, 229, 231

Shelter 19, 194, 217

Shepherds 62, 125

Shield 30, 65, 125, 144, 209, 213

Sick 56, 148, 165, 216, 221

Silence 176, 220, 222, 227, 238

Silver platter 14, 84, 124, 147, 171

Simple 14, 19, 25, 52, 57, 63, 72, 84, 85

Sin 20, 54, 59, 103, 109

Sing 14, 21, 47, 90, 120, 143, 145, 170, 187, 198, 217, 229

Sinner 59

Sins 59, 69, 80, 93, 95, 103, 197, 221

Sister 67, 109, 112

Skills 14, 34, 73, 74, 75, 79, 86, 90, 106, 107, 112, 151, 152, 180, 184, 189, 198, 199, 207, 209, 232

Skype 148

Skyscrapers 224

Slander 207

Slaughter 38, 67, 80, 100, 198

Slaughtered 58, 198

Slave 67, 86, 135, 140, 163, 210, 215

Smile 39, 44, 45, 65, 139, 186, 199, 213

Social 86, 101, 108, 133

Society 9, 10, 23, 32, 40, 58, 62, 67, 72, 78, 80, 86, 87, 90, 93, 94, 96, 101, 106, 107, 108, 109, 113, 114, 118, 119, 120, 122, 123, 128, 129, 147, 151, 152, 156, 158, 162, 163, 165, 166, 167, 171, 176, 177, 178, 179, 180, 184, 187, 193, 201, 202, 204, 209, 210, 215, 216, 221, 223, 225, 227, 229, 232, 233, 234

Soft 124, 171, 175

Soldier 26, 116, 210

Soldiers 26, 54, 68, 116, 118, 209, 210

Solomon 240

Solutions 198

Solve 16, 53, 59, 68, 132, 184, 198,

230

Someone 1, 12, 13, 14, 16, 17, 19, 20, 24, 54, 56, 57, 66, 67, 68, 71, 77, 78, 108, 123, 156, 157, 162, 165, 168, 171, 185, 204, 205, 217, 220, 224, 225

Sometimes 15, 25, 32, 43, 51, 53, 66, 77, 79, 124, 125, 128, 141, 148, 157, 163, 173, 179, 184, 189, 199, 233

Son iii, ix, 14, 51, 54, 112, 145, 147, 180, 185, 186, 189, 191, 209, 213, 222

Song of freedom 134

Song of humanity 229

Songs 21, 170, 221

Soul viii, 12, 20, 23, 29, 56, 58, 59, 66, 81, 87, 101, 104, 108, 137, 140, 141, 142, 145, 155, 164, 186, 193, 194, 197, 199, 201, 202, 204, 213, 214, 221, 231

Space 217

Special 75, 85, 101, 142

Spirit 20, 51, 84, 94, 123, 153, 214

Spirit of GOD 103

Spiritual 30, 56, 103, 167, 216, 228

Sportsman x, 219

Stand ix, 26, 33, 43, 75, 89, 118, 124, 132, 140, 151, 163, 170, 174, 188, 205, 213, 227, 238

Stars 114, 124, 209

Start 15, 22, 56, 65, 84, 101, 106, 147, 164, 189, 193, 194

Status quo 32, 65, 80, 119, 122, 177, 178, 207, 209, 213, 230

Step 12, 24, 46, 64, 80, 83, 86, 102, 122, 139, 153, 184, 185, 192, 194, 200, 207

Steps 20, 22, 25, 27, 36, 52, 53, 56, 109, 173, 177, 199, 214, 220, 237

stereotypes 208

stiff-necked 23

Stirred 52, 96

Storm 1, 73, 185, 186, 189, 209, 217

Storms 11, 33, 43, 44, 51, 89, 125, 180, 204

Strange 32, 33, 42, 55, 61, 65, 69, 88, 159, 171, 200

Stranger 1, 66

Strategies 176

Strategy 22, 189

Straw 173

Strengths 140, 175, 220

Stress iii, 51, 175

Strong 9, 32, 54, 58, 62, 80, 101, 159, 170, 187, 223

Struggle 1, 11, 24, 147, 214

Student 30, 38, 41, 43, 108, 136, 151, 152, 218, 230

Stupid 13, 25, 44, 57, 102, 118, 134, 230, 231

Subconscious 215

Succeed 17, 54, 77, 79, 86, 128, 145, 157, 201

Success 9, 54, 77, 79, 85, 100, 119, 124, 151, 165, 173, 176, 180, 186, 192, 204, 209, 220, 223, 232

Successful 57, 95, 113, 172, 173, 184, 232

Suffer 85, 142, 157, 232

Suicidal 147, 180

Sulphur 63, 64

Sun 18, 20, 90, 96, 148

Supermen 147

Super wives 50

Suppress 1

Surround 78

Survival 10, 18, 19, 29, 71, 86, 119, 132, 158, 163, 171

Survive 9, 18, 27, 32, 75, 108, 114, 133, 166, 173, 177, 179, 202, 215, 222, 224, 225

Swallow 1, 14

Sword 17, 102, 148, 153, 173, 188,

189, 220
Sycophancy 183
Sympathy 193
System i, 39, 40, 73, 87, 103, 119, 128, 221

# T

Talent 61, 165, 190, 192, 193, 220
Talents 36, 151, 190, 198
Taxes 73, 108
Tea 55, 231
Teach 15, 20, 23, 30, 37, 41, 73, 100, 124, 163, 200, 205, 220
Teacher 27, 30, 31, 33, 38, 73, 89, 96, 152, 177, 188, 194, 205, 230
Teachers 15, 22, 33, 50, 54, 98, 100, 145, 235
Teacher's reward 37
Teaching 12, 73, 85, 102
Tears 13, 36, 37, 38, 47, 67, 87, 89, 90, 95, 100, 101, 125, 143, 147, 192, 199, 209, 215, 217, 227, 230, 237
Technology 151
Temple 14, 20, 51, 104, 134, 193, 197
Temporal power 202, 215
Tempted 58, 188
Tent 4, 18, 61, 98, 109, 145, 194, 221, 235
Terrorists 149
Tested 33, 58, 176, 188, 222, 224
The Bluffer 24
the LORD GOD ALMIGHTY 240
The self 124, 152
Thieves 18, 108, 207
Think positive 77
Thirst 172
Thoughts 11, 29, 61, 65, 69, 80, 103, 109, 195, 197, 208
Threat 91, 122, 123, 162, 177, 232
Threatened 68, 77, 132, 147
Throne ix, 21, 71, 74, 93, 124, 136,

142, 169, 176, 183, 189, 228, 236
Thrones 57, 187, 223
Thugs 207
Time 9, 14, 16, 22, 23, 26, 29, 30, 33, 34, 37, 38, 39, 40, 42, 43, 47, 50, 52, 54, 56, 58, 61, 64, 65, 78, 83, 84, 86, 90, 94, 96, 103, 104, 107, 113, 114, 119, 120, 122, 124, 125, 129, 132, 140, 141, 143, 144, 145, 148, 151, 152, 156, 157, 158, 162, 164, 165, 168, 171, 173, 175, 176, 179, 184, 188, 189, 193, 194, 197, 198, 200, 208, 213, 214, 215, 217, 218, 222, 223, 227, 228, 229, 230, 232, 235, 238
Timing 189
Titans 187
Tomorrow iv, v, 9, 10, 12, 13, 23, 26, 29, 35, 42, 51, 77, 120, 172, 177, 178, 181, 210, 211, 221
Tongue 58, 85, 100, 141, 145, 170, 175, 221, 231
Tools 32, 158
Top 55, 141, 144, 168, 170, 175, 184, 189, 205, 222
Toughness 199
Toys 157
Trading 133
Tragedy 100, 120, 214
Train 163, 164, 194, 207
Training 33, 144, 193
Traitors 129, 172
Transform 165
Transformation 42, 156
Trap 59, 106, 171
Trapped ix, 18, 45, 179, 193, 203, 227
Traps 42, 53, 114
Trees 109, 134, 136
Trials 16, 129, 158, 178, 209
Triumph 17, 59, 77, 87, 139, 160, 178
Troubles 16, 39, 186, 216, 232

True vii, 1, 10, 29, 30, 31, 32, 36, 57,
    62, 68, 73, 77, 95, 102, 105,
    106, 109, 124, 125, 128, 133,
    134, 136, 140, 143, 216, 222,
    234, 235
Trust 15, 17, 22, 45, 65, 100, 115, 133,
    172, 217
Trusted 41, 52, 53, 94, 133
Truth x, 1, 2, 23, 29, 30, 31, 44, 47,
    61, 66, 75, 83, 84, 89, 101, 102,
    120, 136, 144, 158, 197, 212,
    215, 217, 218, 230, 233, 234
Tyrant 59, 222

Village 216
Villains 52, 74, 233
Virtues 66, 101, 123, 139, 163
Vision 12, 34, 125, 179, 186, 228, 230
Visionaries 118
Visions 33, 188
Voice vii, 10, 15, 17, 20, 25, 29, 31, 41,
    42, 54, 69, 85, 86, 88, 91, 96,
    100, 104, 105, 106, 112, 125,
    129, 140, 156, 175, 179, 184,
    192, 193, 204, 223, 227, 230,
    232
Vultures 143, 186

## U

Ultimate weapon 30, 45, 159, 163
Unbearable 59, 71, 202
Uncertainty 186, 234
Unity 86, 101, 139, 204
Universe v, 8, 39, 52, 64, 69, 128, 129,
    238
Unknown 11, 71
Unlimited 62, 64, 107
Untamed 101
Upward 83, 170

## V

Valley 97, 170, 173, 207
Values 15, 17, 40, 56, 58, 80, 86, 87,
    108, 120, 162, 163, 165, 199,
    202, 228, 234
Vanity 66, 104, 108, 122, 159, 177,
    216, 220, 228, 230
Vectors 17
Vegetables 55
Vengeance 19, 68, 89
Victories 21, 199, 228
Victory 21, 26, 42, 98, 122, 176, 178,
    207, 228, 233
Viewpoints 231

## W

Wait 37, 180, 184, 217
Walls 87, 102, 144, 166, 216
War 16, 22, 26, 30, 41, 47, 53, 54, 64,
    65, 81, 83, 84, 98, 115, 118,
    120, 135, 141, 147, 152, 153,
    173, 178, 187, 200, 207, 209,
    233, 235
War and Anarchy 234
Warfare 55
Warrior 17, 19, 22, 26, 71, 148, 164,
    176, 199, 233, 235
Warriors 2, 234
Wars 18, 31, 36, 54, 71, 135, 141, 147,
    217, 228, 233, 234, 235
War zones 83
Waste 15, 19, 55, 61, 62, 65, 73, 112,
    115, 144, 159, 209
Watch 20, 29, 52, 120, 158, 177, 199,
    217
Watches 17, 27, 38, 52, 176
Weak 9, 12, 41, 56, 67, 94, 96, 176,
    224
Weakness 94, 128, 158, 186, 221
Wealth iii, v, viii, ix, 8, 11, 12, 16, 22,
    36, 52, 56, 57, 59, 72, 73, 88,
    91, 93, 94, 104, 108, 113, 120,
    125, 129, 130, 133, 136, 144,

153, 159, 162, 167, 169, 173, 181, 183, 197, 215, 216, 220, 225

Wealthy 132, 179, 188, 216

Weapons 17, 19, 26, 30, 71, 81, 123, 135, 144, 145, 149, 179, 200, 223, 229

WhatsApp 148

Wicked 29, 53, 102, 183

Wickedness 18, 53, 93, 144, 220

Wife iii, 86, 101, 125, 148, 188, 202, 213

Will i, ix, 44, 56, 63, 112, 122, 133, 143, 178, 179, 184, 189, 192, 196, 200, 222, 224, 237

Win 67, 83, 98, 122, 141, 147, 207

Wing 38

Wings 1, 22, 24, 134, 145

Winners 57, 233

Wisdom 1, 9, 11, 12, 16, 17, 22, 25, 27, 36, 37, 39, 42, 43, 44, 51, 53, 54, 57, 59, 61, 62, 63, 67, 72, 91, 96, 109, 114, 120, 125, 129, 135, 136, 143, 152, 153, 158, 159, 162, 163, 166, 167, 175, 178, 187, 189, 198, 200, 201, 208, 209, 214, 216, 218, 227, 232

Wise viii, 11, 15, 20, 21, 23, 27, 30, 36, 41, 45, 48, 51, 58, 59, 61, 62, 63, 64, 65, 67, 68, 71, 72, 73, 77, 83, 85, 95, 96, 100, 106, 107, 112, 120, 124, 125, 128, 131, 132, 141, 151, 158, 159, 162, 166, 167, 179, 181, 184, 185, 192, 193, 194, 197, 200, 201, 202, 204, 208, 214, 220, 222, 228, 230, 231, 232

Wishes 23, 43, 56, 222

Wives 50, 88

Woe 62, 73, 95, 100, 167

Woman 25, 41, 44, 45, 68, 125, 126, 145, 183, 227, 229

Women 50, 183, 223, 234

Word 31, 42, 74, 170

Words 3, 14, 17, 19, 21, 39, 42, 43, 52, 53, 58, 59, 65, 67, 77, 95, 100, 113, 115, 120, 128, 136, 139, 145, 162, 167, 176, 183, 184, 192, 207, 213, 217, 218, 220, 223, 238

Words of God 42

Work iii, iv, 14, 15, 20, 23, 29, 32, 38, 40, 46, 61, 77, 78, 79, 94, 101, 102, 106, 108, 113, 141, 143, 157, 162, 167, 168, 171, 172, 175, 188, 189, 202, 213, 215, 220, 233, 235

World ii, iv, 1, 9, 12, 17, 20, 22, 30, 31, 33, 37, 38, 39, 42, 44, 45, 47, 50, 51, 53, 54, 55, 56, 61, 63, 66, 67, 69, 71, 74, 77, 85, 90, 94, 95, 96, 97, 102, 103, 108, 109, 114, 115, 123, 124, 125, 128, 129, 134, 135, 136, 139, 140, 141, 142, 144, 145, 149, 151, 153, 154, 159, 167, 170, 171, 177, 180, 184, 185, 187, 192, 194, 199, 202, 210, 215, 216, 217, 223, 224, 225, 228, 231, 232, 233, 235

Worlds 30, 52, 54, 66, 69, 71, 88, 115, 126, 141, 153, 200, 210, 215, 216, 235

World trade 224

Worries 47, 61, 113

Worship 34, 45, 77, 95, 125, 149

Worthy 43

Wounds 24, 202, 221

Wrath 62, 75, 96

Write 75, 188

Wrong 25, 71, 95, 122, 128, 156, 165, 185, 213, 224

# Y

YAHWEH  87
Yashua  187
Young  13, 66, 128, 165, 180, 209
Yourself  vi, vii, 14, 18, 19, 20, 21, 22, 24, 25, 32, 54, 58, 66, 67, 68, 71, 72, 78, 80, 84, 86, 99, 102, 107, 108, 109, 115, 120, 121, 125, 135, 144, 147, 156, 157, 158, 166, 167, 170, 171, 172, 175, 176, 180, 185, 186, 189, 193, 194, 197, 199, 205, 207, 208, 209, 215, 222, 228, 229, 230, 231, 232
Youth  39, 72, 96, 100, 101, 107, 108, 120, 124, 163, 175, 180, 190, 223, 225, 226, 231
Youthfulness  73, 120, 220

www.ingramcontent.com/pod-product-compliance
Lightning Source LLC
Chambersburg PA
CBHW071333280526
45787CB00001B/81